THE SOCIETY
of the
CROSSED KEYS

SELECTIONS FROM THE WRITINGS OF

STEFAN ZWEIG

Translated by Anthea Bell

**PUSHKIN
PRESS**

Pushkin Press
71–75 Shelton Street, London WC2H 9JQ

'A Conversation with Wes Anderson'
© Wes Anderson and George Prochnik 2014

The World of Yesterday first published in German as
Die Welt von Gestern in 1942
This translation first published by Pushkin Press in 2009
English translation © Anthea Bell 2009

Beware of Pity first published in German as
Ungeduld des Herzens in 1939
This translation first published by Pushkin Press in 2011
English translation © Anthea Bell 2011

Twenty-four Hours in the Life of a Woman first published in German as
Vierundzwanzig Stunden aus dem Leben einer Frau in 1927
This translation first published by Pushkin Press in 2003
English translation © Anthea Bell 2003

First published by Pushkin Press in 2014
003

ISBN 978 1 782271 07 9

Set in Monotype Baskerville by Tetragon, London
Printed in Great Britain by CPI Group (UK)

www.pushkinpress.com

CONTENTS

—

A CONVERSATION WITH
WES ANDERSON

Wes Anderson is an American director and screenwriter. His films include *Bottle Rocket, Rushmore, The Royal Tenenbaums, The Life Aquatic, The Darjeeling Limited, Fantastic Mr Fox*, and *Moonrise Kingdom*. He directed and wrote the screenplay for *The Grand Budapest Hotel*, his latest film.

George Prochnik is the author of *The Impossible Exile: Stefan Zweig at the End of the World*. He is editor-at-large for *Cabinet* magazine.

———

GEORGE PROCHNIK: I thought your film did a beautiful job of transposing Stefan Zweig's actual life into the dream life of his stories, and the stories into the fabric of his actual life. You showed how deeply implicated they were in one another—not in the sense that Zweig was necessarily writing directly about his own experiences, but in the way his own experiences had a fairy-tale dimension, confectionary and black by turns. This dream-like aspect of his work and existence seem central to understanding him. I wondered if you could say anything about these qualities and how Zweig became an inspiration for you.

WES ANDERSON: One thing that struck me, after I had read a few of Zweig's books, is that what I began to learn about him personally was quite different from what I *felt* I understood about him from his voice as a writer. So much of his work is written from the point of view of someone who's quite innocent and is entering into kind of darker territories, and I always felt that Zweig himself was a more reserved person who was exploring things in his work that he was drawn to but that weren't his own experiences. In fact, the truth seems to be completely the opposite. He seems to be somebody who more or less tried everything along the way.

PROCHNIK: I agree, and I'm curious whether this quality of Zweig's character resonates with the intriguing title you gave this collection, *The Society of the Crossed Keys*.

ANDERSON: Well, that just refers to a little made-up secret guild of European hotel concierges in our movie. Many of the ideas expressed and/or explored in *Grand Budapest* we stole directly from Zweig's own life and work; and then, also, maybe the membership of the Society itself might hint at hidden, secret corners of Zweig's world which we are only now starting to pull back the curtains on.

I had never heard of Zweig—or, if I had, only in the vaguest ways—until maybe six or seven years ago, something like that, when I just more or less by chance bought a copy of *Beware of Pity*. I loved this first book, and immediately there were dozens more in front of me that hadn't been there before. They were all suddenly back in print. I also read the *The Post Office Girl*, which had been only published for the first time recently. *The Grand Budapest Hotel* has elements that were sort of stolen from both these books. Two characters in our story are vaguely meant to represent Zweig himself—our "Author" character, played by Tom Wilkinson, and the theoretically fictionalised version of himself, played by Jude Law. But, in fact, M. Gustave, the main character who is played by Ralph Fiennes, is modelled significantly on Zweig as well.

PROCHNIK: Zweig's stories are always nesting stories within stories and confessional revelations of deep secrets within secrets. The action of observing other people's secrets becomes the occasion for personal disclosures by the observer. The way that your film seems to work on that grid of multiple overlapping and proliferating story lines was very striking.

ANDERSON: We see this over and over again in Zweig's short stories. It's a device that maybe is a bit old-fashioned—I feel it's the kind of thing we might expect to find in something by Conrad or Melville—where somebody meets an interesting, mysterious person and there's a bit of scene that unfolds with them before they eventually settle down to tell their whole tale, which then becomes the larger book or story we're reading. I love that in Zweig—you describe it as confessional, and they *do* have that feeling, and they're usually secret. One of his novellas is even called *Burning Secret*. Anyway, that sort of technique is such an effective way to set the stage, to set a mood. It draws you in before you say, "Now I will tell you my story." It creates this kind of a "gather around" feeling.

PROCHNIK: When you were speaking about the device as a convention, I was thinking also about Freud. You probably know that Zweig was a good friend of Freud's—and a huge admirer of his theories. There's one letter Freud wrote Zweig in which he praises Zweig's work and remarks that there's an astonishing quality to his novellas whereby they seem to grope closer and closer to the most intimate inner core of their subject matter, the way that symbols accumulate in a dream. This idea calls to mind as well what you did with Zweig and his work. Reading his fictions I often feel that while on the one hand they're formalised and traditional, there's also something so peculiar and subverted.

ANDERSON: I agree. There's a word I use to describe it, which is "psychological". When I've occasionally said that to describe Zweig I always want to say, Now, what do you mean by that? Because I don't really know what I mean by this. But the stories feel psychological. It feels like there are contradictions within the characters that are being explored and there's something unconscious that's always brewing, and the behaviour that people don't really want anyone to know about is kind of forcing its way into view.

PROCHNIK: I think that's exactly right. There's a strange, compulsive quality to that process of revelation. And whatever the psychological quality to his fiction is, it definitely has something to do with the unconscious. He was so concerned with states of complete immersion and concentration, like the powerful moment in his memoir when he describes watching Rodin begin to touch up a sculpture he's working on and forgetting that Zweig is even there in the studio with him. Zweig was fascinated by fascination—losing yourself in that way. I think when his fictions work you can feel him going after some kindred process.

ANDERSON: Like the state in which he worked. He liked absolute quiet and seclusion in his work—this was a particular issue for him—and I could see that need for silence tying into this. Think about the novella *Confusion*. Zweig is both of the main characters there. Because I can see the student who kind of goes off the rails in Berlin and enters into this wild life as one aspect of Zweig's experience; and then there's the academic, who's sort of distant, and whose relationship with his wife is full of secrets. I feel he's represented in both these characters. I mean I guess that's probably normal. Writers are inside all kinds of characters.

PROCHNIK: But I think the split is particularly true to his nature. Many of Zweig's friends characterised his social persona as that of the voyeur who would never quite take part in the dance-hall action—he would sit there and watch. But then at the same time there are odd stories about him—for example of his possibly having been a flasher when he was a young man. There were rumours that Zweig used to go to a park in Vienna and expose himself. And Freud of course saw these kinds of desires on the same axis—that need to expose oneself and to be hidden he saw as very linked.

ANDERSON: There are other stories by Zweig I think of that might relate to this as well. There's the story where a guy starts going to red light districts in a Kasbah-type place each night—*Moonbeam Alley*. And that's very similar to what he describes the student in *Confusion* doing when he arrives in Berlin. And I think these experiences in his fiction relate for me to that chapter of *The World of Yesterday* where Zweig describes how totally repressed they were as students in Vienna, and how as a result of that everything was secret. There was so much going on that was secretive. Everything sexual was illicit—and so there were loads of whorehouses and things, and it was all on that hidden level.

PROCHNIK: Secret chambers in restaurants, and so on. You know, that chapter in *The World of Yesterday*, "Eros Matutinus," which I was very happy to see you've made one of the selections for this book, is considered by some scholars to be the most historically original part of what he wrote. The kind of taxonomy of the sexual underworld of *fin de siècle* Vienna Zweig creates there is almost without parallel. There's an amazing letter that Zweig wrote near the end of his life, just after he'd finished revising *The World of Yesterday* in Brazil, where he describes the entire book to a friend as "a hard and realistic image of sexuality in our youth." He ends up converging everything on that one chapter, which was only added when he was in Brazil. It was an afterthought. He had written a whole draft of the memoir while he was living in Ossining, up the river from New York City, and then he adds that one chapter, almost like his own secret, that he couldn't divulge until the very end.

ANDERSON: Very interesting. It makes sense that he would see it that way afterwards. My experience of reading the book was full of that sense of surprising realities being disclosed.

It was the thing that struck me the most. There were so many descriptions of parts of life, which—as much as we may have read or seen something of them in movies—we didn't *really* know about from his time, before reading Zweig's memoir. In particular I don't think I ever thought about the moment when it became necessary to have a passport, which is hugely meaningful when you see it through his eyes. You suddenly see this control that comes in.

PROCHNIK: I think it was absolutely devastating for him—that loss of geographical freedom, the ability to just cross borders without thinking about it. Zweig was addicted to that sense of access to novelty and heterogeneity in culture and individuals. He was so deeply invested in idiosyncrasy of every sort and there's just a sense of everything gradually becoming more monotone and congealed. I thought you also did a lovely job of depicting this transformation in the film, near the end, where you have the extraordinary scene in which your protagonists are stopped a final time on the train for their papers and it's clear just how vital these documents have become—a matter of life and death.

ANDERSON: You can see why for Zweig this turn of events would be the beginning of everything that became too much to bear. Not only because he was someone who had friends all over Europe and collected people actively—made friendships and made these connections and so on. He also collected manuscripts and books and musical scores, and he was gathering things from all over—among artists he admired. And eventually all this, plus his own work, was taken away, destroyed, made impossible for him to continue pursuing in that way. And when you read *The World of Yesterday* you just see how all the things he invested his life in, this world that he prefers to call the world of security, this life that had been growing more and more refined and free that's so meaningful to him, is just obliterated.

PROCHNIK: There were friends of Zweig who saw him as invested before the war in creating almost a cabinet of curiosities, a museum of Europe—one person described it as a garden—that would serve as a microcosm of the whole vast continent before it all got blown asunder.

ANDERSON: Vienna—the environment he grew up in was so—I guess, art was the centre of his own activity, and it was also the popular thing. One detail that I remember from *The World of Yesterday* is that the daily newspapers they got each morning had poetry and philosophical writings. He and his friends went to meet in cafés regularly in groups. And there were new plays continuously being produced, and they were all following these playwrights. Vienna was a place where there was this great deep culture, but it was the equivalent of rock stars—it was the coolest thing of the moment. It was completely popular, and that was Vienna. Zweig was living in the dead centre, ground zero place for this. And he was living there up to the point that it came to an end.

PROCHNIK: One passage that always strikes me in *The World of Yesterday* is when he begins to talk about what's happened to the news, and how it's suddenly just become—in a way this seems to foreshadow our own world—a kind of nonstop disaster feed. Zweig talks about that moment when suddenly the wireless is working, and you're getting reports of catastrophes in China, and wars in countries that you don't know anything about. You're enveloped in a present-ness that is all about the most sensational, most dispiriting acts of bloodthirstiness and natural catastrophe that really seem to suck away the reflective element that had been part of newspapers when he was young.

ANDERSON: Ideas and thoughts. Not just accounts of terrible events. I think one thing that Zweig does very simply, that just seems so clear to him, is that he attributes everything that's gone wrong to nationalism, and the two ideologies of socialism slash communism and fascism. These two movements might be conflicting, but to him they were just equally disastrous—

PROCHNIK: To the individual.

ANDERSON: Yes, these dogmas take hold so forcefully or forcibly that it's just the beginning of the end, and he sees it happen right in front of him. Because of the monolithic nature of them. I think there were all kinds of aspects of socialism he would have embraced. But the problem for him was that people began to identify themselves with these dogmas, and then people began to oppose each other on the basis of these causes or dogmatic kind of movements.

PROCHNIK: After the First World War Vienna had arguably the most progressive government in Europe—a socialist government, and people came from everywhere to study the model. Zweig was certainly sympathetic to that. It wasn't something that he advertised about himself, but I'm sure he would have considered his politics from an economic perspective to be in accord with socialism.

I want to cycle back to his fictions. When you said that *Beware of Pity* was really your introduction to Zweig—why did you find this work to be so compelling?

ANDERSON: As we discussed, the book takes a form that we sort of overtly lifted for our movie, and I particularly loved the opening scene. There's a wonderful brief introduction from the author, and then it goes back some years, and we see the author who's visiting a restaurant that he thought would have fallen out of fashion a long time ago, outside Vienna. But then he's sort of surprised that he's still seeing people he knows there and this figure—this guy comes over to him, a guy he knows vaguely. (This author character is well-known, he's famous like Zweig.) And the guy who comes over to him he describes as the sort of person who knows everybody, at least a bit, and bounces around among people and table hops and name drops. It's a very familiar sort of person today. You know immediately you can connect him to a few people who you might know and even like, but who do this.

PROCHNIK: I love the phrase that Zweig has for this type— which translates literally from the German as "Also-present" ("hanger-on" in translation).

ANDERSON: And the author character has this moment with him. He's a little unhappy to see him—he wanted to be alone—but at the same time it's not so bad, and now he has somebody to talk to. And then that "Also-present" figure sees a man across the room our author does not recognise, but then he tell him the man's name, and the author knows exactly who he's talking about: he's a war hero. And then

18

the author and the war hero reconnect by chance at a party the next day, and this time they actually meet. They talk about that guy who was bouncing around the restaurant, and they click. That whole set up to me is the best. First, it's happening in a setting that is very interesting to me—this Vienna that is unfamiliar and exotic, and at the same time there's so much that I do feel connected to: that it could be happening in some place like Manhattan today. There are the same kinds of people and dynamics we know from our world. But also details of a universe most of us have no experience of, and that's great to discover. I remember being gripped by Zweig's description of the cavalry unit that the lead character is a part of. There's great detail about that whole way of life. But then we're pulled into this story very, very quickly. We plunge into an account of what happens to him with a family that he makes a kind of social success with, and who he then gets drawn into a strange, complicated, disastrous relationship with.

PROCHNIK: A relationship centred around a sort of warped pity—this whole fascinating double definition of pity that Zweig gives at the outset, that's really at the core of what the book is trying to explore. There's pity that's meant just to exonerate the person expressing it from actually having to deal with the object of their pity—and then there's another kind of pity, that consumes the whole being of the compassionate person as he or she tries to merge in solidarity with the object of pity right to the end, and beyond.

ANDERSON: Yes, and at each step the novel's protagonist tries to do the right thing, and at the same time his motivations are a little bit complicated; but everything he does, even while it may rescue the situation for a moment, actually ends by digging him in deeper and deeper and deeper. And the other thing that happens is that this book leads up to the war. It was shortly after finishing *Beware of Pity* that I started reading *The World of Yesterday*. You see how this moment is reflected over and over again in his work.

PROCHNIK: Yes, and it's so surprising that the scenes in the introduction you pointed to—in a restaurant and at a party where things feel very civilised and very social—the reader then discovers are happening in 1938. So it's five years after Hitler has been appointed Chancellor, the same year as the annexation of Austria, and one year before everything goes completely to hell. With this whole book, Zweig manages to take the very personal story of a minor officer's increasingly engrossing and twisted relationship as a metaphor for our greater human inability to stop digging ourselves deeper into the grave as cultural entities beyond our individual fates.

ANDERSON: Yes, it's a great book. It's his biggest fiction work by far. It's the only real novel, and it's just a masterpiece. When I read it I thought, how is it that I don't already know about this—how is it that I seem to be the only person I know who's read this book? At that time I really had not heard anything about it from anybody.

PROCHNIK: When I was first reading Zweig, I had a similar experience where I would ask very educated friends of mine in the United States about him, and none of them knew who he was. Part of what really got me also to write a book about him was the sense that his erasure was so violent. I came to know slightly Zweig's step niece, the niece of Lotte, his second wife, who is a wonderful woman living in London. I remember at one point she told me that he thought he would be completely forgotten. Zweig predicted so many aspects of his own undoing and even disappearance. He was aware of the contingency to his whole project.

ANDERSON: To be erased in his mother tongue…There's the story of the libretto for the opera he wrote for Richard Strauss after the Nazis had come to power in Germany— *The Silent Woman*. And the premiere was in Dresden, and then what happened?

PROCHNIK: Strauss kept insisting on Zweig's participation and the use of his name in the programme, even though Jews weren't really allowed by this point to be part of cultural productions of any sort, let alone something on this scale. Strauss was the head of music in the Reich. He was an incredibly powerful person within the bureaucracy. And he argued that Zweig's participation was crucial for the opera's success. The opera did in fact open and it was enormously successful. Immediately there were bookings in multiple cities around the Reich—and at that point they just shut the whole thing down, they just pulled the cloth off the table.

But it's not only erasure in the mother tongue. There's an amazing moment in Zweig's life in the spring of 1941 when he was in New York City. PEN in Exile was just in formation at time, and there was an enormous launch banquet given at the Biltmore Hotel. Something like a thousand writers were supposed to be there. Many people gave speeches, and Zweig's proved to be the one that got the most attention. In a completely counterintuitive move, Zweig came out and said, I'm here to apologise before you all. I'm here in a state of shame because my language is the language in which the world is being destroyed. My mother tongue, the very words that I speak, are the ones being twisted and perverted by this machine that is undoing humanity.

ANDERSON: He thought his language itself had been permanently distorted.

PROCHNIK: And felt a personal responsibility for this as a German-writing, -speaking man of letters.

ANDERSON: One thing I thought of along the way—just in how his own psychology is revealed through is work—one thing you do see all along with Zweig is these suicides. People commit suicide, people talk about suicide regularly all through his body of work, and it's a bit eerie for us now. Whatever you read first, the one thing you do know—even the shortest bio on a dust jacket of Zweig tells you how it ends. And it's something that really jumps out at you when you come across it, which isn't so infrequent.

PROCHNIK: It's there in so many of his works, and the larger culture had a frighteningly high suicide rate as well. There seems to have been some kind of psychological, sociocultural implosion that people were sensitive to. In his last years, Zweig was strikingly given to repeatedly saying, Europe is committing suicide—actually using these words. The whole continent is committing suicide.

ANDERSON: At one point he also refers to the suicide of our independence: the choice people are making, without realising it, to destroy their own freedom.

PROCHNIK: There's an amazing essay Zweig wrote in the 1920s called 'The Monotonisation of the World'. It's essentially a critique of the global exporting of American mass culture. He writes how Europe took the first step toward destroying itself in the First World War. And the second stage is Americanisation, whereby everyone everywhere takes up mass fashion, mass sport, mass dance crazes, mass cinema. This homogenisation he equated with the destruction of independence you mentioned—people fighting to destroy their own individuality, really, out of a desire to be part of these different collective crazes of which he saw America as the wellspring.

ANDERSON: Zweig saw this as a kind of American invention. Making popular movements so successful, sweeping up so many people in them—I mean, I guess America is just that way.

PROCHNIK: The whole essay feels weirdly prescient of the critiques we see today. I do want to ask you also about the choice of including the whole of that extraordinary novella *Twenty-four Hours in the Life of a Woman*, which has its own suicide. What was it that drew you to that work in particular?

ANDERSON: Well it was also one of the first ones I read. One of the first of his short stories I came upon. Zweig conjures up the experience of this French resort of the past so vividly there, and this woman. He uses the same storytelling technique again. He sets the stage with a whole circle of people who are responding to something happening among them, a sort of scandal happening among them, but eventually that's not what this story is about. That's just a sort of prelude. And I loved that form. And then I was also taken with how this person who you get to know on the surface as an older person is so clearly drawn. And when she finally tells her own story that image is completely broken, and you realise how thoroughly you did *not* know her and her history. Some of Zweig's short stories have been done as whole films, and I think that this one—you could see Max Ophüls doing *Twenty-four Hours in the Life of a Woman* and making a masterpiece.

PROCHNIK: With all of the despair in Zweig's stories and life, he shows us again and again that there were just a hell of a lot of splendid spots around Europe to go to and to spend time in. Even in the little sketches he gives, there's something so visually charismatic in just the suggestion of what these places were. We somehow feel an aura of that luminous life—

ANDERSON: That luxury.

PROCHNIK: You really show that compellingly. You did an amazing job of revealing how parts of the fairy tale were real in the landscapes—and the hotels of course.

ANDERSON: One thing we came across as we were trying to figure where to do this movie was a collection of images on the US Library of Congress website. There's this thing, the Photochrom Collection. Two different companies—one Swiss and one American—had a sort of joint venture, where they took black-and-white photographs all over the world, and then they colourised them and mass-produced them. And there are thousands of them. They're from maybe 1895 to 1910, something like that, all over the Austro-Hungarian Empire, and Prussia, and all over the world. I compare it to the Google Earth of the turn of the century. These are almost all landscapes and cityscapes. There are places that are just known as views. There are many, many of these spots where you can see a little terrace that's been created, just because people would walk to this place and look out. It's wonderful, and it really influenced our movie. There's a wonderful photochrom of the hotel that I always thought of as sort of the model for our hotel, which is the Hotel Pupp in Karlovy Vary, which was Carlsbad. The thing we learned when we visited all sorts of places that we found on this collection of pictures was that none of them were enough like what they once were to work for us. But the photochrom images seemed to tap into a truth about Zweig's vision of the world that I was able to draw on in developing a visual aura for the film.

In *The Post Office Girl*, Zweig's description of the grand hotel in Switzerland is so evocative. The protagonist is a girl who works in the post office. She's invited to stay in this hotel as a gift from her rich aunt, and when she arrives in this place, the management thinks she's there to make a delivery. Her suitcase is a basket. Finally they realise she's actually going to be a guest in the hotel, which is unlike anywhere she's ever been. Her point of view about this treatment she receives, and her experience of walking in and realising, "This is where I'm going to sleep", is so powerful. But also that by the time her holiday abruptly ends, she is already addicted to this other way of life, and her existence is so dramatically changed, and a sort of desperation comes over her—and then a connection she makes with someone who is in his own desperate state. The idea of that work being something that had been out of print for that long is sort of surreal.

PROCHNIK: I agree. This idea—that a brief exposure to how good life can be was a fatal infection, in terms of the social order of that time—is rendered so powerfully. The notion that really, when life was good in pre-War Europe, it could be awfully sweet. But it's interesting—when you described going around looking for a place in the real world to film, and not finding one, I thought also of the sentiment expressed near the end of your film, when the possibility is raised that the world M. Gustave inhabits may really have ceased to exist even before he entered it. There is the suggestion that the whole thing is a feat of imagination. I think this resonates with the embrace of illusion in *The World of Yesterday*. It gets away from the idea that Zweig was just unable to see reality, and moves more towards the notion that he just had a huge desire to live in the imagination so fully that it would diminish the impact of the real.

ANDERSON: That's a good one! That might be a good ending.

FEBRUARY 2014

From

THE WORLD OF YESTERDAY
Selections from the memoirs
of Stefan Zweig

THE WORLD OF SECURITY

Reared as we are, in quiet and in peace,
Now all at once we're thrown upon the world.
Thousands of waves wash round us without cease,
Often delighted, sometimes pleased, we're whirled
From joy to grief, and so from hour to hour
Our restless feelings waver, change and sway.
Our senses know a strange, tumultuous power,
And in the turmoil find no place to stay.

GOETHE

I F I TRY TO FIND some useful phrase to sum up the time
of my childhood and youth before the First World War,
I hope I can put it most succinctly by calling it the Golden
Age of Security. Everything in our Austrian Monarchy, then
almost a thousand years old, seemed built to last, and the state
itself was the ultimate guarantor of durability. The rights it
gave its citizens were affirmed by our parliament, a freely
elected assembly representing the people, and every duty
was precisely defined. Our currency, the Austrian crown,
circulated in the form of shiny gold coins, thus vouching for
its own immutability. Everyone knew how much he owned and

what his income was, what was allowed and what was not. Everything had its norm, its correct measurement and weight. If you had wealth, you could work out precisely how much interest it would earn you every year, while civil servants and officers were reliably able to consult the calendar and see the year when they would be promoted and the year when they would retire. Every family had its own budget and knew how much could be spent on food and lodging, summer holidays and social functions, and of course you had to put a small sum aside for unforeseen contingencies such as illness and the doctor. If you owned a house you regarded it as a secure home for your children and grandchildren; property in town or country was passed on from generation to generation. While a baby was still in the cradle, you contributed the first small sums to its way through life, depositing them in a money box or savings account, a little reserve for the future. Everything in this wide domain was firmly established, immovably in its place, with the old Emperor at the top of the pyramid, and if he were to die the Austrians all knew (or thought they knew) that another emperor would take his place, and nothing in the well-calculated order of things would change. Anything radical or violent seemed impossible in such an age of reason.

This sense of security was an asset owned by millions, something desirable, an ideal of life held in common by all. Life was worth living only with such security, and wider and wider circles were eager to have their part in that valuable asset. At first only those who already owned property enjoyed advantages, but gradually the population at large came to aspire to them. The era of security was also the golden age of the insurance industry. You insured your house against fire and theft, your land against damage by storms and hail, your body against accidents and sickness; you bought annuities for your old age; you put insurance policies in your girl children's cradles to provide their future dowries. Finally even the working classes organised themselves to demand a certain level of wages as the norm, as well as health insurance schemes. Servants saved for their old age, and paid ahead of time into policies for their own funerals. Only those who could look forward with confidence to the future enjoyed the present with an easy mind.

But for all the solidity and sobriety of people's concept of life at the time, there was a dangerous and overweening pride in this touching belief that they could fence in their existence, leaving no gaps at all. In its liberal idealism, the nineteenth century was honestly convinced that it was on the direct and infallible road to the best of all possible worlds. The people of the time scornfully looked down on earlier epochs with their wars, famines and revolutions as periods when mankind had not yet come of age and was insufficiently enlightened. Now, however, it was a mere matter of decades before they finally saw an end to evil and violence, and in those days this faith in uninterrupted, inexorable 'progress' truly had the force of a religion. People believed in 'progress' more than in the Bible, and its gospel message seemed incontestably proven by the new miracles of science and technology that were revealed daily. In fact a general upward development became more and more evident, and at the end of that peaceful century it was swift and multifarious. Electric lights brightly lit the streets by night, replacing the dim lamps of the past; shops displayed their seductive new brilliance from the main streets of cities all the way to the suburbs; thanks to the telephone, people who were far apart could speak to each other; they were already racing along at new speeds in horseless carriages, and fulfilling the dream of Icarus by rising in the air. The comfort of upper-class dwellings now reached the homes of the middle classes; water no longer had to be drawn from wells or waterways; fires no longer had to be laboriously kindled in the hearth; hygiene was widespread, dirt was disappearing. People were becoming more attractive, stronger, healthier, and now that there were sporting activities to help them keep physically fit, cripples, goitres and mutilations were seen in the streets less and less frequently. Science, the archangel of progress, had worked all these miracles. Social welfare was also proceeding apace; from year to year more rights were granted to the individual, the judiciary laid down the law in a milder and more humane manner, even that ultimate problem, the poverty of the masses, no longer seemed insuperable. The right to vote was granted to circles flung wider and wider, and with it the opportunity for voters to defend their own interests legally. Sociologists and professors competed to make the lives of the proletariat healthier and even happier—no wonder that century basked in its own sense of achievement and regarded every decade, as it drew to a close, as the prelude to an even better one. People no more believed in the possibility of barbaric relapses, such as wars between the nations of Europe, than they believed in ghosts and witches; our fathers were doggedly convinced of the infallibly binding power of tolerance and conciliation.

They honestly thought that divergences between nations and religious faiths would gradually flow into a sense of common humanity, so that peace and security, the greatest of goods, would come to all mankind.

Today, now that the word 'security' has long been struck out of our vocabulary as a phantom, it is easy for us to smile at the optimistic delusion of that idealistically dazzled generation, which thought that the technical progress of mankind must inevitably result in an equally rapid moral rise. We who, in the new century, have learnt not to be surprised by any new outbreak of collective bestiality, and expect every new day to prove even worse than the day just past, are considerably more sceptical about prospects for the moral education of humanity. We have found that we have to agree with Freud, who saw our culture and civilisation as a thin veneer through which the destructive forces of the underworld could break at any moment. We have had to accustom ourselves slowly to living without firm ground beneath our feet, without laws, freedom or security. We long ago ceased believing in the religion of our fathers, their faith in the swift and enduring ascent of humanity. Having learnt our cruel lesson, we see their overhasty optimism as banal in the face of a catastrophe that, with a single blow, cancelled out a thousand years of human effort. But if it was only a delusion, it was a noble and wonderful delusion that our fathers served, more humane and fruitful than today's slogans. And something in me, mysteriously and in spite of all I know and all my disappointments, cannot quite shake it off. What a man has taken into his bloodstream in childhood from the air of that time stays with him. And despite all that is dinned into my ears daily, all the humiliation and trials that I myself and countless of my companions in misfortune have experienced, I cannot quite deny the belief of my youth that in spite of everything, events will take a turn for the better. Even from the abyss of horror in which we try to feel our way today, half-blind, our hearts distraught and shattered, I look up again and again to the ancient constellations that shone on my childhood, comforting myself with the inherited confidence that, some day, this relapse will appear only an interval in the eternal rhythm of progress onward and upward.

Now that a great storm has long since destroyed it, we know at last that our world of security was a castle in the air. Yet my parents lived in it as if it were a solid stone house. Not once did a storm or a cold draught invade their warm, comfortable existence. Of course they had special protection from cold winds; they were prosperous people who grew rich, then even very rich, and wealth comfortably draught-proofed your windows and walls in those times. Their way of life seems to me typical of the Jewish middle classes that had made significant contributions to Viennese culture, only to be exterminated root and branch by way of thanks, and I can say impersonally of their comfortable and quiet existence that, in that era of security, ten or twenty thousand Viennese families lived just as my parents did.

My father's family came from Moravia. The Jewish communities there lived in small country towns and villages, on excellent terms with the peasants and the lower middle classes. They felt none of the sense of oppression suffered by the Jews of Galicia further to the east, nor did they share their impatience to forge ahead. Made strong and healthy by life in the country, they walked the fields in peace and security, just as the peasants of their native land did. Emancipated at an early date from orthodox religious observance, they were passionate supporters of the contemporary cult of 'progress', and in the political era of liberalism they provided parliament with its most respected deputies. When they moved from their places of origin to Vienna, they adapted with remarkable speed to a higher cultural sphere, and their personal rise was closely linked to the general economic upswing of the times. Here again, my family was entirely typical in its development. My paternal grandfather had sold manufactured goods. Then, in the second half of the century, came the industrial boom in Austria. Mechanical looms and spinning machines imported from Britain rationalised manufacturing, bringing a great reduction in costs by comparison with traditional handloom weaving, and Jewish businessmen, with their gift for commercial acumen and their international perspective, were the first in Austria to recognise the necessity of switching to industrial production and the rewards it would bring. Usually beginning with only a small capital sum, they founded swiftly erected factories, initially driven by water power, which gradually expanded to become the mighty Bohemian textiles industry that dominated all Austria and the Balkans. So while my grandfather, a middleman dealing in ready-made products, was a typical representative of the previous generation, my father moved firmly into the modern era at the age of thirty-three by founding a small weaving mill in northern Bohemia. Over the years, he slowly and carefully built it up into a business of considerable size.

Such caution in expanding the business, even when the economic situation looked enticingly favourable, was very much in the spirit of the times. It also exactly suited my father's reserved and far from avaricious nature. He had taken the 'safety first' creed of his epoch as his own watchword; it was more important to him to own a sound business (the ideal of something sound and solid was also characteristic of the period), with the force of his own capital behind it, than to extend it to huge dimensions by taking out bank loans and mortgages. The one thing of which he was truly proud was that no one had ever in his life seen his name on a promissory note, and he had never failed to be in credit with his bank—which of course was the soundest bank of all, the Kreditanstalt founded by the Rothschilds. Any kind of transaction carrying the faintest suggestion of risk was anathema to him, and he never in all his years took part in any foreign business dealings. The fact that he still gradually became rich, and then even richer, was not the result of bold speculation or particularly farsighted operations, but of adapting to the general method of that cautious period, expending only a modest part of his income and consequently, from year to year, making an increasingly large contribution to the capital of the business. Like most of his generation, my father would have considered anyone who cheerfully spent half his annual income without thought for the future a dubious wastrel at the very least. Providing for the future was another recurrent idea in that age of security. Steadily setting profits aside meant rising prosperity.

In addition, the state had no plans to take more than a few per cent of even the largest incomes in taxes, while state and industrial securities brought in good rates of interest, so that making money was quite a passive process for the well-to-do. And it was worth it; the savings of the thrifty were not stolen, as they are during times of inflation; no pressure was put on sound businesses, and even those who were particularly patient and refrained from any kind of speculation made good profits. Thanks to adapting to the general system of his time, in his fifties my father could be regarded as a very prosperous man by international standards. But the lifestyle of our family lagged well behind the increasingly rapid rise of its property. We did gradually acquire small comforts. We moved from a small apartment to a larger one, we hired a car for outings on spring afternoons, we travelled second class by train and booked a sleeper, but it was not until he was fifty that my father first allowed himself the luxury of taking my mother to Nice for a month in the winter. All things considered, he stuck to his basic attitude of enjoying wealth by knowing that he had it, rather than by making a great display of it. Even as a millionaire, my father never smoked any imported product but—like Emperor Franz Joseph with his cheap Virginia tobacco—the ordinary Trabuco cigars of the time, and when he played cards it was only for small stakes. He inflexibly maintained his restraint and his comfortable but discreet way of life. Although he was very much better educated than most of his colleagues, and culturally superior to them—he played the piano extremely well, wrote a good, clear hand, spoke French and English—he firmly declined any distinctions or honorary positions, and

37

never in his life either aspired to or accepted any honour or dignity of the kind frequently offered to him in his position as a leading industrialist. His secret pride in never having asked anyone for anything, never having been obliged to say 'please' or 'thank you', meant more to him than any outward show.

There inevitably comes a moment in every man's life when he sees his father reflected in himself. That preference for privacy, for an anonymous way of life, is beginning to develop in me more and more strongly as the years go by, though in fact it runs contrary to my profession, which is bound to make my name and person to some extent public. But out of the same secret pride as his, I have always declined any form of outward honour, never accepted any decoration or title, or the presidency of any association. I have never been a member of an academy, nor have I sat on the board of any company or on any jury panel. Attending a festive occasion is something of an ordeal for me, and the mere thought of asking someone a favour is enough—even if my request were to be made through a third party—to make my mouth dry up before uttering the first word. I know that such inhibitions are out of tune with the times, in a world where we can remain free only through cunning and evasion, and where, as Goethe wisely said, "in the general throng, many a fool receives decorations and titles." But my father in me, with his secret pride, makes me hold back, and I cannot resist him. After all, it is my father I have to thank for what I feel is, perhaps, my one secure possession: my sense of inner freedom.

*

My mother, whose maiden name was Brettauer, was not of the same origin. Hers was an international family. She was born in Ancona in Italy, and Italian and German had both been the languages of her childhood. When she was discussing something with her mother, my grandmother or her sister, and they did not want the servants to know what they were saying, they would switch to Italian. From my earliest youth I was familiar with risotto, artichokes (still a rarity in Vienna at the time) and the other specialities of Mediterranean cookery, and whenever I visited Italy later I immediately felt at home. But my mother's family was not by any means Italian, and saw itself as more cosmopolitan than anything else. The Brettauers, who had originally owned a bank, came from Hohenems, a small town on the Swiss border, and spread all over the world at an early date on the model of the great Jewish banking families, although of course on a much smaller scale. Some went to St Gallen, others to Vienna and Paris. My grandfather went to Italy, an uncle to New York, and these international contacts gave the family more sophistication, a wider outlook, and a certain arrogance. There were no small tradesmen in the family, no brokers, they were all bankers, company directors, professors, lawyers and medical doctors; everyone spoke several languages, and I remember how naturally the conversation around my aunt's table in Paris moved from one language to another. It was a family that thought well of itself, and when a girl from one of its poorer branches reached marriageable age, everyone contributed to providing her with a good dowry so that she need not marry 'beneath herself'. As a leading industrialist, my father was respected, but my mother, although theirs was the happiest of marriages, would never have allowed his relations to consider themselves the equals of hers. It was impossible to root out the pride of their descent from a 'good family' from the Brettauers, and in later years, if one of them wanted to show me particular goodwill, he would condescend to say, "You're more of a Brettauer really", as if stating approvingly that I took after the right side of my family.

This kind of distinction, claimed for themselves by many Jewish families, sometimes amused and sometimes annoyed my brother and me, even as children. We were always hearing that certain persons were 'refined', while others were less so. Enquiries were made about any new friends of ours—were they from a 'good family'?—and every ramification of their origins in respect of both family and fortune was investigated. This constant classification, which was in fact the main subject of all family and social conversations, seemed to us at the time ridiculous and snobbish, since after all, the only difference between one Jewish family and another was whether it had left the ghetto fifty or a hundred years ago. Only much later did I realise that this idea of the 'good family', which seemed to us boys the farcical parody of an artificial pseudo-aristocracy, expresses one of the most mysterious but deeply felt tendencies in the Jewish nature. It is generally assumed that getting rich is a Jew's true and typical aim in life. Nothing could be further from the truth. Getting rich, to a Jew, is only an interim stage, a means to his real end, by no means his aim in itself. The true desire of a Jew, his inbuilt ideal, is to rise to a higher social plane by becoming an intellectual. Even among Orthodox Eastern Jews, in whom the failings as well as the virtues of the Jewish people as a whole are more strongly marked, this supreme desire to be an intellectual finds graphic expression going beyond merely material considerations—the devout Biblical scholar has far higher status within the community than a rich man. Even the most prosperous Jew would rather marry his daughter to an indigent intellectual than a merchant. This high regard for intellectuals runs through all classes of Jewish society, and the poorest pedlar who carries his pack through wind and weather will try to give at least one son the chance of studying at university, however great the sacrifices he must make, and will consider it an honour to the entire family that one of them is clearly regarded as an intellectual: a professor, a scholar, a musician. It is as if such a man's achievements ennobled them all. Unconsciously, something in a Jew seeks to escape the morally dubious, mean, petty and pernicious associations of trade clinging to all that is merely business, and rise to the purer sphere of the intellect where money is not a consideration, as if, like a Wagnerian character, he were trying to break the curse of gold laid on himself and his entire race. Among Jews, then, the urge to make a fortune is nearly always exhausted within two or at most three generations of a family, and even the mightiest dynasts find that their sons are unwilling to take over the family banks and factories, the prosperous businesses built up and expanded by the previous generation. It is no coincidence that Lord Rothschild became an ornithologist, one of the Warburgs an art historian, one of the Cassirer family was a philosopher, one of the Sassoons a poet; they were all obeying the same unconscious urge to liberate themselves from the mere cold earning of money that has restricted Jewish life, and perhaps this flight to the intellectual sphere even expresses a secret longing to exchange their Jewish identity for one that is universally human. So a 'good' family means more than a mere claim to social status; it also denotes a Jewish way of life that, by adjusting to another and perhaps more universal culture, has freed itself or is freeing itself from all the drawbacks and constraints and pettiness forced upon it by the ghetto. Admittedly, it is one of the eternal paradoxes of the Jewish destiny that this flight into intellectual realms has now, because of the disproportionately large number of Jews in the intellectual professions, become as fatal as their earlier restriction to the material sphere.[1]

In hardly any other European city was the urge towards culture as passionate as in Vienna. For the very reason that for centuries Austria and its monarchy had been neither politically ambitious nor particularly successful in its military ventures, native pride had focused most strongly on distinction in artistic achievement. The most important and valuable provinces of the old Habsburg empire that once ruled Europe—German and Italian, Flemish and Walloon—had seceded long ago, but the capital city was still intact in its old glory as the sanctuary of the court, the guardian of a millennial tradition. The Romans had laid the foundation stones of that city as a *castrum*, a far-flung outpost to protect Latin civilisation from the barbarians, and over a thousand years later the Ottoman attack on the West was repelled outside the walls of Vienna. The Nibelungs had come here, the immortal Pleiades of music shone down on the world from this city, Gluck, Haydn and Mozart, Beethoven, Schubert, Brahms and Johann Strauss, all the currents of European culture had merged in this place. At court and among the nobility and the common people alike, German elements were linked with Slavonic, Hungarian, Spanish, Italian, French and Flemish. It was the peculiar genius of Vienna, the city of music, to resolve all these contrasts harmoniously in something new and unique, specifically Austrian and Viennese. Open-minded and particularly receptive, the city attracted the most disparate of forces, relaxed their tensions, eased and placated them. It was pleasant to live here, in this atmosphere of intellectual tolerance, and unconsciously every citizen of Vienna also became a supranational, cosmopolitan citizen of the world.

This art of adaptation, of gentle and musical transitions, was evident even in the outward appearance of the city. Growing slowly over the centuries, developing organically from its centre, with its two million inhabitants Vienna had a large enough population to offer all the luxury and diversity of a metropolis, and yet it was not so vast that it was cut off from nature, like London or New York. The buildings on the edge of the city were reflected in the mighty waters of the Danube and looked out over the wide plain, merged with gardens and fields or climbed the last gently undulating green and wooded foothills of the Alps. You hardly noticed where nature ended and the city began, they made way for one another without resistance or contradiction. At the centre, in turn, you felt that the city had grown like a tree, forming ring after ring, and instead of the old ramparts of the fortifications, the Ringstrasse enclosed the innermost, precious core with its grand houses. In that core, the old palaces of the court and the nobility spoke the language of history in stone; here Beethoven had played for the Lichnowskys; there Haydn had stayed with the Esterházys; the premiere of his *Creation* was given in the old university; the Hofburg saw generations of emperors, Napoleon took up residence at Schönbrunn Palace; the united rulers of Christendom met in St Stephen's Cathedral to give thanks for their salvation from the Turks, the university saw countless luminaries of scholarship and science in its walls. Among these buildings the new architecture rose, proud and magnificent, with shining avenues and glittering emporiums. But old Vienna had as little to do with the new city as dressed stone has to do with nature. It was wonderful to live in this city, which hospitably welcomed strangers and gave of itself freely; it was natural to enjoy life in its light atmosphere, full of elation and merriment like the air of Paris. Vienna, as everyone knew, was an epicurean city—however, what does culture mean but taking the raw material of life and enticing from it its finest, most delicate and subtle aspects by means of art and love? The people of Vienna were gourmets who appreciated good food and good wine, fresh and astringent beer, lavish desserts and tortes, but they also demanded subtler pleasures. To make music, dance, produce plays, converse well, behave pleasingly and show good taste were arts much cultivated here. Neither military, political nor commercial matters held first place in the lives of individuals or society as a whole; when the average Viennese citizen looked at his morning paper, his eye generally went first not to parliamentary debates or foreign affairs but to the theatrical repertory, which assumed an importance in public life hardly comprehensible in other cities. For to

44

the Viennese and indeed the Austrians the imperial theatre, the Burgtheater, was more than just a stage on which actors performed dramatic works; it was a microcosm reflecting the macrocosm, a bright mirror in which society could study itself, the one true *cartigiano* of good taste. In an actor at the imperial theatre, spectators saw an example of the way to dress, enter a room, make conversation, were shown which words a man of taste might use and which should be avoided. The stage was not just a place of entertainment but a spoken, three-dimensional manual of good conduct and correct pronunciation, and an aura of esteem, rather like a saint's halo, surrounded all who had even the faintest connection with the court theatre. The Prime Minister, the richest magnate, could walk through the streets of Vienna and no one would turn to stare, but every salesgirl and every cab driver would recognise an actor at the court theatre or an operatic diva. When we boys had seen one of them pass by (we all collected their pictures and autographs) we proudly told each other, and this almost religious personality cult even extended to their entourages; Adolf von Sonnenthal's barber, Josef Kainz's cab driver were regarded with awe and secretly envied. Young dandies were proud to have their clothes made by the tailors patronised by those actors. A notable anniversary in a famous actor's career, or a great actor's funeral, was an event overshadowing all the political news. It was every Viennese dramatist's dream to be performed at the Burgtheater, a distinction that meant a kind of ennoblement for life and brought with it a series of benefits such as free theatre tickets for life and invitations to all official occasions, because you had been a guest in an imperial house.

I still remember the solemn manner of my own reception. The director of the Burgtheater had asked me to visit his office in the morning, where he informed me—after first offering his congratulations—that the theatre had accepted my play. When I got home that evening, I found his visiting card in my apartment. Although I was only a young man of twenty-six, he had formally returned my call; my mere acceptance as an author writing for the imperial stage had made me a gentleman whom the director of that institution must treat as on a par with himself. And what went on at the theatre indirectly affected every individual, even someone who had no direct connection with it whatsoever. I remember, for instance, a day in my earliest youth when our cook burst into the sitting room with tears in her eyes: she had just heard that Charlotte Wolter, the star actress of the Burgtheater, had died. The grotesque aspect of her extravagant grief, of course, lay in the fact that our old, semi-literate cook had never once been to that distinguished theatre herself, and had never seen Charlotte Wolter either on stage or in real life, but in Vienna a great Austrian actress was so much part of the common property of the entire city that even those entirely unconnected with her felt her death was a catastrophe. Every loss, the death of a popular singer or artist, inevitably became an occasion for national mourning. When the old Burgtheater where the premiere of Mozart's *The Marriage of Figaro* had been given was to be demolished, Viennese high society gathered there in a mood of solemn emotion, and no sooner had the curtain fallen than everyone raced on stage to take home at least a splinter from the boards that had been trodden by their favourite artists as a relic. Even

46

decades later, these plain wooden splinters were kept in precious caskets in many bourgeois households, just as splinters of the Holy Cross are preserved in churches.

In my own day, we acted no more rationally when the so-called Bösendorfer Saal was torn down. In itself that little concert hall, which was reserved exclusively for chamber music, was a modest building, not suggesting any great artistic distinction. It had been Prince Liechtenstein's riding school, and was adapted for musical purposes only by the addition of interior boarding, without any ostentation. But it had the resonance of an old violin, and it was a sacred place to music-lovers because Chopin and Brahms, Liszt and Rubinstein had given recitals there, and many of the famous quartets had first performed in this hall. And now it was to make way for a new purpose-built concert hall; such a thing was beyond the understanding of those of us who had spent many memorable hours there. When the last bars of Beethoven died away, played better than ever by the Rosé Quartet, none of the audience left their seats. We shouted and applauded, some of the women were sobbing with emotion, no one was willing to admit that this was goodbye. The lights in the hall were extinguished to clear us out of the place. Still none of the four or five hundred people present left their seats. We stayed for half-an-hour, an hour, as if our presence could save the sacred hall by force. And as students, how we campaigned, with petitions and demonstrations and articles, to keep the house where Beethoven died from demolition! Whenever one of these historic Viennese buildings went, it was as if a part of our souls were being torn from our bodies.

This fanatical love of art, in particular the art of the theatre, was common to all classes of society in Vienna. Its hundreds of years of tradition had made the city itself a place with a clearly ordered and also—as I once wrote myself—a wonderfully orchestrated structure. The imperial house still set the tone, while the imperial palace represented not only the spatial centre of the city but also the supranational nature of the monarchy. Around that palace lay the grand residences of the Austrian, Polish, Czech and Hungarian nobility, forming what might be called a second rampart. Then came the houses of the members of 'good society'—the minor nobility, higher civil servants, captains of industry and the 'old families'. Below them came the lower middle class and the proletariat. All these social classes lived in their own circles and even in their own districts of the city: at the centre the great noblemen in their palaces, the diplomats in District Three, businessmen and industrialists near the Ringstrasse, the lower middle class in the inner districts, Districts Two to Nine, the proletariat on the periphery. However, they all came into contact with each other at the theatre and for major festivities such as the Floral Parade, when three hundred thousand spectators enthusiastically greeted the 'upper ten thousand' in their beautifully decorated carriages. Everything in Vienna that expressed itself in colour or music became an occasion for festivities: religious spectacles like the Corpus Christi procession, the military parades, performances by the outdoor musicians of the Burgmusik, even funerals attracted enthusiastic audiences, and it was the ambition of every true Viennese to end up as 'a handsome corpse' with a fine funeral procession and many companions escorting him on his last journey. A genuine Viennese turned even his death into a fine show for others to enjoy. The entire city was united in this sensitivity to everything colourful, musical and festive, in this delight in theatrical spectacle as a playful reflection of life, whether on the stage or in real space and time.

It was not difficult to make fun of the theatrical mania of the Viennese, whose delight in tracking down the tiniest details of the lives of their favourites sometimes became grotesque, and our Austrian political indolence and economic backwardness, by comparison with the determined German Reich next door, may indeed be partly ascribed to our overrating of sensuous pleasure. But in cultural terms the very high value placed on the arts created something unique—a great veneration for all artistic achievement, leading over the centuries to unequalled expertise, and finally, thanks in its own turn to that expertise, to outstandingly high standards in all cultural fields. An artist always feels most at ease and at the same time most inspired in a place where he is valued, even overvalued. Art always reaches its zenith where it is important in the life of an entire nation. And just as Renaissance Florence and Rome attracted painters and trained them to achieve greatness, because every one of them felt bound to keep outdoing others and himself, competing in front of the citizens as a whole, so musicians and actors knew how important they were in Vienna. At the Opera House, in the Burgtheater, nothing was overlooked, every wrong note was instantly detected, every incorrect entry or abridged passage deplored, and this keen surveillance was exercised not only by professional critics at premieres, but day after day by the alert ear of the public at large, honed as

49

it was by constant comparison. While the attitude in politics, the administration and morality was easygoing, and one made allowances for a slipshod piece of work and showed leniency for an offence, no quarter was given in artistic matters. Here the honour of the city was at stake. Every singer, every actor, every musician must constantly give of his best, or his career was finished. It was wonderful to be a darling of the public in Vienna, but it was not easy to maintain that position. No lowering of standards was forgiven. And this awareness of being under constant and pitiless observation forced every artist in Vienna to do his best, bringing the art of the city as a whole to a very high level. All of us who lived there in our youth have brought a stern and implacable standard of artistic performance into our lives from those years. Those who saw discipline exercised down to the smallest detail at the Opera House under Gustav Mahler, and vitality combined with meticulous accuracy taken as the norm in music played by the Philharmonic, are rarely entirely satisfied with theatrical or musical performances today. But we also learnt to criticise our own artistic performance; the example before us was, and still is, a high level of achievement inculcated into rising artists in few other cities in the world. This understanding of the right rhythm and momentum went deep into the people themselves, for even the most unassuming citizen sitting over his *Heurige*,[2] demanded good music from the wind band just as he expected good value from the landlord. Similarly, people knew exactly which military band played with most verve in the Prater, whether it was the German Masters or the Hungarians. Anyone who lived in Vienna absorbed a sense of rhythm as if it were in the air. And just as that musicality expressed itself in writers in the particular attention we paid to writing particularly well-turned prose, in others the sense of delicacy was expressed in social attitudes and daily life. In what was known as 'high society', a Viennese with no appreciation of art or pleasure in form was unimaginable, but even among the lower classes the lives of the poorest showed a certain feeling for beauty drawn from the surrounding landscape and genial human attitudes. You were not truly Viennese without a love for culture, a bent for both enjoying and assessing the prodigality of life as something sacred.

For Jews, adaptation to the human or national environment in which they lived was not only a measure taken for their own protection, but also a deeply felt private need. Their desire for a homeland, for peace, repose and security, a place where they would not be strangers, impelled them to form a passionate attachment to the culture around them. And nowhere else, except for Spain in the fifteenth century, were such bonds more happily and productively forged than in Austria. Here the Jews who had been settled in the imperial city for over two hundred years met people who took life lightly and were naturally easygoing, while under that apparently light-hearted surface they shared the deep Jewish instinct for intellectual and aesthetic values. And the two came together all the more easily in Vienna, where they found a personal task waiting for them, because over the last century Austrian art had lost its traditional guardians and protectors: the imperial house and the aristocracy. In the eighteenth century Maria Theresia had had her daughters taught the pleasures of music, Joseph II had discussed Mozart's operas with him as a connoisseur, Leopold II was a composer himself, but the later emperors Franz II and Ferdinand had no kind of interest in art, and Emperor Franz Joseph, who in his eighty years of life never read or even picked up a book other than the Army List, even felt a decided antipathy to music. Similarly, the great noblemen had abandoned their former position as patrons; gone were the glorious days when the Esterházys gave house-room to Haydn, when the Lobkowitzes and Kinskys and Waldsteins competed for the first performance of a work by Beethoven to be given in their palaces, when Countess Thun went on her knees to that great daemonic figure asking him not to withdraw *Fidelio* from the Opera. Even Wagner, Brahms, Johann Strauss and Hugo Wolf no longer received the slightest support from them; the citizens of Vienna had to step into the breach to keep up the old high standard of the Philharmonic concerts and enable painters and sculptors to make a living, and it was the particular pride and indeed the ambition of the Jewish bourgeoisie to maintain the reputation of Viennese culture in its old brilliance. They had always loved the city, taking it to their hearts when they settled there, but it was their love of Viennese art that had made them feel entirely at home, genuinely Viennese. In fact they exerted little influence otherwise in public life; the lustre of the imperial house left all private wealth in the shade, high positions in the leadership of the state were in hereditary hands, diplomacy was reserved for the aristocracy, the army and the higher reaches of the civil service for the old-established families, and the Jews did not even try to look so high as to force their way into those privileged circles. They tactfully respected such traditional privileges as something to be taken for granted. I remember, for instance, that my father never in his life ate at Sacher's, not for reasons of economy—the price difference between Sacher and the other great hotels was ridiculously small—but out of a natural instinct for preserving a distance. He would have felt it embarrassing or unseemly to sit at the table next to one occupied by, say, Prince Schwarzenberg or Prince Lobkowitz. It was only in art that all the Viennese felt they had equal rights, because art, like love, was regarded as a duty incumbent on everyone in the city, and the part played by the Jewish bourgeoisie in Viennese culture, through the aid and patronage it offered, was immeasurable. They were the real public, they filled seats at the theatre and in concert halls, they bought books and pictures, visited exhibitions, championed and encouraged new trends everywhere with minds that were more flexible, less weighed down by tradition. They had built up virtually all the great art collections of the nineteenth century, they had made almost all the artistic experiments of the time possible. Without the constant interest of the Jewish bourgeoisie as stimulation, at a time when the court was indolent and the aristocracy and the Christian millionaires preferred to spend money on racing stables and hunts rather than encouraging art, Vienna would have lagged as far behind Berlin artistically as Austria did behind the German Reich in politics. Anyone wishing to introduce a novelty to Vienna, anyone from outside seeking understanding and an audience there, had to rely on the Jewish bourgeoisie. When a single attempt was made in the anti-Semitic period[3] to found a so-called National Theatre, there were no playwrights or actors or audiences available; after a few months the 'National Theatre' failed miserably, and that example first made it clear that nine-tenths of what the world of the nineteenth century celebrated as Viennese culture was in fact culture promoted and nurtured or even created by the Jews of Vienna.

For in recent years the Viennese Jews—like those of Spain before their similarly tragic downfall—had been artistically creative, not in any specifically Jewish style but, with miraculous empathy, giving especially intense expression to all that was Austrian and Viennese. As composers, Goldmark, Gustav Mahler and Schönberg were figures of international stature; Oscar Straus, Leo Fall and Kálmán brought the traditional waltz and operetta to new heights; Hofmannsthal, Arthur Schnitzler, Beer-Hofmann and Peter Altenberg gave Viennese literature new status in Europe, a rank that it had never before reached even at the time of Grillparzer and Stifter. Sonnenthal and Max Reinhardt revived the international reputation of Vienna as a city of the theatre; Freud and the great scientific experts attracted attention to the famous and ancient university—everywhere, as scholars, virtuoso musicians, painters, directors, architects, journalists, they claimed high and sometimes the highest positions in the intellectual life of Vienna. Through their passionate love of the city and their adaptability they had become entirely assimilated, and were happy to serve the reputation of Austria; they felt that the assertion of their Austrian identity was their vocation.

In fact, it must be said in all honesty that a good part, if not the greater part, of all that is admired today in Europe and America as the expression of a newly revived Austrian culture in music, literature, the theatre, the art trade, was the work of the Jews of Vienna, whose intellectual drive, dating back for thousands of years, brought them to a peak of achievement. Here intellectual energy that had lost its sense of direction through the centuries found a tradition that was already a little weary, nurtured it, revived and refined it, and with tire-less activity injected new strength into it. Only the following decades would show what a crime it was when an attempt was made to force Vienna—a place combining the most hetero-geneous elements in its atmosphere and culture, reaching out intellectually beyond national borders—into the new mould of a nationalist and thus a provincial city. For the genius of Vienna, a specifically musical genius, had always been that it harmonised all national and linguistic opposites in itself, its culture was a synthesis of all Western cultures. Anyone who lived and worked there felt free of narrow-minded prejudice. Nowhere was it easier to be a European, and I know that in part I have to thank Vienna, a city that was already defending universal and Roman values in the days of Marcus Aurelius, for the fact that I learnt early to love the idea of community as the highest ideal of my heart.

We lived well, we lived with light hearts and minds at ease in old Vienna, and the Germans to the north looked down with some annoyance and scorn at us, their neighbours on the

Danube who, instead of being capable and efficient like them and observing strict principles of order, indulged themselves, ate well, enjoyed parties and the theatre, and made excellent music on those occasions. Instead of cultivating German efficiency, which finally embittered and destroyed the lives of all other peoples, instead of the greedy will of Germany to rise supreme and forge a way forward, we Viennese loved to chat at our ease; we liked pleasant social gatherings, and in a kindly and perhaps lax spirit of concord we let all have their share without grudging it. 'Live and let live' was famous as a Viennese principle, a principle that still seems to me more humane than any categorical imperative, and it reigned supreme in all social circles. Poor and rich, Czechs and Germans, Christians and Jews lived peacefully together in spite of the occasional needling remark, and even political and social movements did not have that terrible spitefulness that eventually made its way into the bloodstream of the time as a poisonous residue of the First World War. In the old Austria you fought chivalrously; you might complain in the newspapers and parliament, but then the deputies, after delivering their Ciceronian tirades, would sit happily together over coffee or a beer, talking on familiar terms. Even when Lueger, leader of the anti-Semitic party,[4] became mayor of the city, nothing changed in private social relationships, and I personally must confess that I never felt the slightest coldness or scorn for me as a Jew either in school, at the university, or in literature. Hatred between country and country, nation and nation, the occupants of one table and those of another, did not yet leap to the eye daily from the newspaper, it did not divide human beings from other human beings, nations from other nations. The herd instinct of the mob was not yet as offensively powerful in public life as it is today; freedom in what you did or did not do in private life was something taken for granted—which is hardly imaginable now—and toleration was not, as it is today, deplored as weakness and debility, but was praised as an ethical force.

For I was not born into a century of passion. It was a well-ordered world with a clear social structure and easy transitions between the parts of that structure, a world without haste. The rhythm of the new speed had not yet transferred itself from machinery, the motor car, the telephone and the aeroplane to humanity. Time and age were judged by different criteria. People lived a more leisurely life, and when I try to picture the figures of the adults who played a large part in my childhood it strikes me how many of them grew stout before their time. My father, my uncle, my teacher, the salesmen in shops, the musicians in the Philharmonic at their music desks were all portly, 'dignified' men at the age of forty. They walked slowly, they spoke in measured tones, and in conversation they stroked their well-groomed beards, which were often already grey. But grey hair was only another mark of dignity, and a 'man of mature years' deliberately avoided the gestures and high sprits of youth as something unseemly. Even in my earliest childhood, when my father was not yet forty, I cannot remember ever seeing him run up or down a staircase, or indeed do anything in visible haste. Haste was not only regarded as bad form, it was in fact superfluous, since in that stable bourgeois world with its countless little safeguards nothing sudden ever happened. Those disasters that did take place on the periphery of our world did not penetrate the well-lined walls of our secure life. The Boer War, the Russo-Japanese War, even the Balkan Wars did not make any deep impression on my parents' lives. They skimmed all the war reporting in the paper as indifferently as they looked at the sports headlines. And what, indeed, did anything that happened outside Austria have to do with them, what change did it bring to their lives? In the serene epoch of their Austria, there was no upheaval in the state, no abrupt destruction of their values. Once, when securities fell by four or five points on the stock exchange, it was called a 'crash' and discussed with furrowed brow as a catastrophe. People complained of high taxes more out of habit that from any real conviction, and by comparison with those of the post-war period the taxes then were only a kind of little tip you gave the state. The most precise stipulations were laid down in wills for ways to protect grandsons and great-grandsons from any loss of property, as if some kind of invisible IOU guaranteed safety from the eternal powers, and meanwhile people lived comfortably and tended their small worries like obedient domestic pets who were not really to be feared. When an old newspaper from those days happens to fall into my hands, and I read the excitable reports of some small local council election, when I try to remember the plays at the Burgtheater with their tiny problems, or think of the disproportionate agitation of our youthful debates on fundamentally unimportant matters, I cannot help smiling. How Lilliputian all those anxieties were, how serene that time! The generation of my parents and grandparents was better off, they lived their lives from one end to the other quietly in a straight, clear line. All the same, I do not know whether I envy them. For they drowsed their lives away remote from all true bitterness, from the malice and force of destiny; they knew nothing about all those crises and problems that oppress the heart but at the same time greatly enlarge it. How little they knew, stumbling along in security and prosperity and comfort, that life can also mean excess and tension, constant surprise, can be turned upside down; how little they guessed in their touching liberal optimism that every new day dawning outside the window could shatter human lives. Even in their darkest nights they never dreamt how dangerous human beings can be, or then again how much power they can have to survive dangers and surmount trials. We who have been hunted through the rapids of life, torn from our former roots, always driven to the end and obliged to begin again, victims and yet also the willing servants of unknown mysterious powers, we for whom comfort has become an old legend and security, a childish dream, have felt tension from pole to pole of our being, the terror of something always new in every fibre. Every hour of our years was linked to the fate of the world. In sorrow and in joy we have lived through time and history far beyond our own small lives, while they knew nothing beyond themselves. Every one of us, therefore, even the least of the human race, knows a thousand times more about reality today than the wisest of our forebears. But nothing was given to us freely; we paid the price in full.

NOTES

1   Zweig is referring to the ban imposed by Hitler's anti-Semitic regime
    on Jews in 'the intellectual professions'. They were no longer, for
    instance, allowed to practise as lawyers and doctors.
2   The wine of the new season's vintage.
3   The National Socialist regime, dating from Hitler's accession to
    power as Chancellor in 1933.
4   Karl Lueger, 1844-1910, leader of the Austrian Christian Socialist
    party. Although he did hold anti-Semitic opinions, he was generally
    regarded as a good mayor of Vienna. Zweig returns to him later in
    this chapter.

EROS MATUTINUS

D URING THOSE EIGHT YEARS at grammar school, one
very personal fact affected us all—starting as children
of ten, we gradually became sexually mature young people
of sixteen, seventeen, eighteen. Nature began to assert its
rights. These days, the awakening of puberty seems to be an
entirely private matter, to be dealt with for themselves by all
young people as they grow up, and it does not at first glance
appear at all suitable for public discussion. For our generation,
however, the crisis of puberty reached beyond its own real
sphere. At the same time, it brought an awakening in another
sense—it taught us to look more critically, for the first time,
at the world of the society in which we had grown up and
its conventions. Children and even adolescents are generally
inclined to conform respectfully to the laws of their environment at first. But they submit to the conventions enjoined
upon them only as long as they see everyone else genuinely
observing them. A single instance of mendacity in teachers or
parents will inevitably make the young turn a distrustful and
thus a sharper eye on their surroundings as a whole. And it did
not take us long to discover that all those authorities whom we
had so far trusted—school, the family, public morality—were

remarkably insincere on one point—the subject of sexuality. Worse than that, they wanted us, too, to dissimulate and cover up anything we did in that respect.

The fact is that thirty or forty years ago, thinking on such subjects was not what it is in the world of today. Perhaps there has never been such a total transformation in any area of public life within a single human generation as here, in the relationship between the sexes, and it was brought about by a whole series of factors—the emancipation of women, Freudian psychoanalysis, cultivation of physical fitness through sport, the way in which the young have claimed independence. If we try to pin down the difference between the bourgeois morality of the nineteenth century, which was essentially Victorian, and the more liberal uninhibited attitudes of the present, we come closest, perhaps, to the heart of the matter by saying that in the nineteenth century the question of sexuality was anxiously avoided because of a sense of inner insecurity. Previous eras which were still openly religious, in particular the strict puritanical period, had an easier time of it. Imbued by a genuine conviction that the demands of the flesh were the Devil's work, and physical desire was sinful and licentious, the authorities of the Middle Ages tackled the problem with a stern ban on most sexual activity, and enforced their harsh morality, especially in Calvinist Geneva, by exacting cruel punishments. Our own century, however, a tolerant epoch that long ago stopped believing in the Devil and hardly believed in God any more, could not quite summon up the courage for such outright condemnation, but viewed sexuality as an anarchic and therefore disruptive force, something that could not be fitted into its ethical system and must not move into the light of day, because any form of extramarital free love offended bourgeois 'decency'. A curious compromise was found to resolve this dilemma. While not actually forbidding a young man to engage in sexual activity, morality confined itself to insisting that he must deal with that embarrassing business by hushing it up. Perhaps sexuality could not be eradicated from the polite world, but at least it should not be visible. By tacit agreement, therefore, the whole difficult complex of problems was not to be mentioned in public, at school, or at home, and everything that could remind anyone of its existence was to be suppressed.

We, who have known since Freud that those who try to suppress natural instincts from the conscious mind are not eradicating them but only, and dangerously, shifting them into the unconscious, find it easy to smile at the ignorance of that naive policy of keeping mum. But the entire nineteenth century suffered from the delusion that all conflicts could be resolved by reason, and the more you hid your natural instincts the more you tempered your anarchic forces, so that if young people were not enlightened about the existence of their own sexuality they would forget it. In this deluded belief that you could moderate something by ignoring it, all the authorities agreed on a joint boycott imposed by means of hermetic silence. The churches offering pastoral care, schools, salons and the law courts, books and newspapers, fashion and custom all on principle avoided any mention of the matter, and to its discredit even science, which should have taken on the task of confronting all problems directly, also agreed to consider that what was natural was dirty, *naturalia sunt turpia*.[1] Science capitulated on the pretext that it was beneath its dignity to study such indecent subjects. Wherever you look in the books of the period—philosophical, legal, even medical—you find that by common consent every mention of the subject is anxiously avoided. When experts on criminal law met at conferences to discuss the introduction of humane practices to prisons and the moral damage done to inmates by life in jail, they scurried timidly past the real central problem. Although in many cases neurologists were perfectly well acquainted with the causes of a number of hysterical disorders, they were equally unwilling to tackle the subject, and we read in Freud how even his revered teacher Charcot admitted to him privately that he knew the real cause of these cases but could never say so publicly. Least of all might any writer of belles-lettres venture to give an honest account of such subjects, because that branch of literature was concerned only with the aesthetically beautiful. While in earlier centuries authors did not shrink from presenting an honest and all-inclusive picture of the culture of their time, so that in Defoe, the Abbé Prévost, Fielding and Rétif de la Bretonne we can still read unvarnished descriptions of the true state of affairs, the nineteenth century saw fit only to show the 'sensitive' and sublime, nothing embarrassing but true. Consequently you will find scarcely a fleeting mention in the literature of that era of all the perils and dark confusions of young city-dwellers of the time. Even when a writer boldly mentioned prostitution, he felt he should refine the subject, presenting a perfumed heroine as the Lady of the Camellias.[2] So we are faced with the strange fact that if young people today, wanting to know how their counterparts of the last couple of generations made their way through life, open the novels of even the great writers of that time, the works of Dickens and Thackeray, Gottfried Keller and Bjørnson,[3] they will find—except in Tolstoy and Dostoevsky, who as Russians stood outside the pseudo-idealism of Europe—accounts of nothing but sublimated, toned-down love affairs because the pressures of the time inhibited that whole generation in its freedom of expression. And nothing more clearly illustrates the almost hysterical over-sensitivity of our forebears' moral sense and the atmosphere in which they lived, unimaginable today, than the fact that even this literary restraint was not enough. Can anyone now understand how such a down-to-earth novel as *Madame Bovary* could be banned by a French court on the grounds of indecency? Or how Zola's novels, in my own youth, could be considered pornographic, or so well-balanced a writer of neoclassical epic works as Thomas Hardy could arouse indignation in England and America? Reserved as they were on the subject, these books had given away too much of the truth.

But we grew up in this unhealthily musty air, drenched with sultry perfumes. The dishonest and psychologically unrealistic morality of covering up sexuality and keeping it quiet weighed down on us in our youth, and as, thanks to the solidarity maintained in this policy of hushing things up, there were no proper accounts available in literature and cultural history, it may not be easy for my readers to reconstruct what had actually happened, incredible as it might seem. However, there is one good point of reference; we need only look at fashion, because the fashions of a period, visibly expressing its tastes, betray its morality. It can be no coincidence that as I write now, in 1940, the entire audience in every town and village all over Europe or America bursts into wholehearted merriment when society men and women of 1900 appear on the cinema screen in the costumes of the time. The most naive of us today will smile at those strange figures of the past, seeing them as caricatures, idiots decked out in unnatural, uncomfortable, unhygienic and impractical clothing. Even we, who saw our mothers, aunts and girlfriends wearing those absurd gowns and thought them equally ridiculous when we were boys, feel it is like a strange dream for a whole generation to have submitted to such stupid costumes without protest. The men's fashions of the time—high, stiff collars, one of them known as the 'patricide', so stiff that they ruled out any ease of movement, the black frock coats with their flowing tails, top hats resembling chimney pipes, also provoke laughter. But most ridiculous of all is a lady of the past in her dress, difficult to put on and hard to wear, every detail of it doing violence to nature. Her body is cut in two at a wasp-waist obtained by a whalebone corset, her skirts billow out in an enormous bell, her throat is enclosed right up to the chin, her feet covered to the toes, her hair piled up into countless little curls and rolls and braids, worn under a majestically swaying monster of a hat, her hands carefully gloved even in the hottest summer—this creature, long ago consigned to history, gives the impression of pitiable helplessness, despite the perfume wafting around her, the jewellery weighing her down and all the costly lace, frills and trimmings. You see at first glance that once inside such garments and invulnerable as a knight in his armour, a woman was no longer free, could not move fast and gracefully, but every movement, every gesture and indeed her whole bearing in such a costume was bound to be artificial and literally unnatural. Merely dressing to look like a lady—never mind all the etiquette of high society—just putting on such gowns and taking them off was a complicated procedure, and impossible without someone else's help. First there were countless little hooks and eyes to be done up behind a lady's back from waist to neck, a maid had to exert all her strength to tight-lace her mistress's corset, her long hair—and let me remind the young that thirty years ago all European women, with the exception of a handful of Russian women students, had hair that fell to their waists when they unpinned it—had to be curled, set, brushed and combed and piled up by a hairdresser called in daily and using a large quantity of hairpins, combs and slides, curling tongs and hair curlers, all this before she could put on her petticoats, camisoles, little bodices and jackets like a set of onion skins, turning and adjusting until the last remnant of her own female form had entirely disappeared. But there was a secret sense in this nonsense. A woman's real figure was to be so entirely concealed by all this manipulation that even at the wedding breakfast her bridegroom had not the faintest idea whether his future companion for life was straight or crooked, plump or thin, had short legs or long legs. That 'moral' age thought it perfectly permissible to add artificial reinforcements to the hair, the bosom and other parts of the body, for the purposes of deception and to conform to the general ideal of female beauty. The more a woman was expected to look like a lady, the less of her natural shape might be shown; in reality the guiding principle behind this fashion was only to obey the general moral tendency of the time, which was chiefly concerned with concealment and covering up.

But that wise morality quite forgot that when you bar the door to the Devil, he usually forces his way in down the chimney or through a back entrance. What strikes our uninhibited gaze today about those costumes, garments so desperately trying to cover every inch of bare skin and hide the natural figure, is not their moral propriety but its opposite, the way that those fashions, provocative to the point of embarrassment, emphasised the polarity of the sexes. While the modern young man and young woman, both of them tall and slim, both beardless and short-haired, conform to each other in easy comradeship even in their outward appearance, in that earlier epoch the sexes distanced themselves from each other as far as possible. The men sported long beards, or at least twirled the ends of a mighty moustache, a clearly recognisable sign of their masculinity, while a woman's breasts, essentially feminine sexual attributes, were made ostentatiously visible by her corset. The extreme emphasis on difference between the so-called stronger sex and the weaker sex was also evident in the attitudes expected of them—a man was supposed to be forthright, chivalrous and aggressive, a woman shy, timid and defensive. They were not equals but hunters and prey. This unnatural tension separating them in their outward behaviour was bound to heighten the inner tension between the two poles, the factor of eroticism, and so thanks to its technique—which knew nothing of psychology, of concealing sexuality and hushing it up—the society of the time achieved exactly the opposite. In its constant prudish anxiety, it was always sniffing out immorality in all aspects of life—literature, art and fashion—with a view to preventing any stimulation, with the result that it was in fact forced to keep dwelling on the immoral. As it was always studying what might be unsuitable, it found itself constantly on the alert; to the world of that time, 'decency' always appeared to be in deadly danger from every gesture, every word. Perhaps we can understand how it still seemed criminal, at that time, for a woman to wear any form of trousers for games or sports. But how can we explain the hysterical prudery that made it improper for a lady even to utter the word 'trousers'? If she mentioned such a sensually dangerous object as a man's trousers at all, she had to resort to the coy euphemism of 'his unmentionables'. It would have been absolutely out of the question for a couple of young people, from the same social class but of different sexes, to go out together by themselves—or rather, everyone's first thought at the mere idea would have been that 'something might happen'. Such an encounter was permissible only if some supervising person, a mother or a governess, accompanied every step that the young people took. Even in the hottest summer, it would have been considered scandalous for young girls to play tennis in ankle-length skirts or even with bare arms, and it was terribly improper for a well-brought-up woman to cross one foot over the other in public, because she might reveal a glimpse of her ankles under the hem of her dress. The natural elements of sunlight, water and air were not permitted to touch a woman's bare skin. At the seaside, women made their laborious way through the water in heavy bathing costumes, covered from neck to ankles. Young girls in boarding schools and convents even had to take baths in long white garments, forgetting that they had bodies at all. It is no legend or exaggeration to say that when women died in old age, their bodies had sometimes never been seen, not even their shoulders or their knees, by anyone except the midwife, their husbands, and the woman who came to lay out the corpse. Today, forty years on, all that seems like a fairy tale or humorous exaggeration. But this fear of the physical and natural really did permeate society, from the upper classes down, with the force of a true neurosis. It is hard to imagine today that at the turn of the century, when the first women rode bicycles or actually ventured to sit astride a horse instead of riding side-saddle, people would throw stones at those bold hussies. Or that, when I was still at school, the Viennese newspapers filled columns with discussions of the shocking innovation proposed at the Opera for the ballerinas to dance without wearing tights. Or that it was an unparalleled sensation when Isadora Duncan, although her style of dancing was extremely classical, was the first to dance barefoot instead of wearing the usual silk shoes under her tunic—which fortunately was long and full. And now think of young people growing up in such an age of watchfulness, and imagine how ridiculous these fears of the constant threat to decency must have appeared to them as soon as they realised that the cloak of morality mysteriously draped over these things was in fact very threadbare, torn and full of holes. After all, there was no getting around the fact that out of fifty grammar school boys, one would come upon his teacher lurking in a dark alley some day, or you heard in the family circle of someone who appeared particularly respectable in front of us, but had various little falls from grace to his account. The fact was that nothing increased and heightened our curiosity so much as this clumsy technique of concealment, and as it was undesirable for natural inclinations to run their course freely and openly, curiosity in a big city created its underground and usually not very salubrious outlets. In all classes of society, this suppression of sexuality led to the stealthy overstimulation of young people, and it was expressed in a childish, inexpert way. There was hardly a fence or a remote shed that was not scrawled with indecent words and graffiti, hardly a swimming pool where the wooden partition marking off the ladies' pool was not full of so-called knotholes through which a peeping Tom might look. Whole industries flourished in secret—industries that have now disappeared because morals and manners are more natural—in particular the trade in nude photographs offered for sale under the counter in bars to adolescent boys. Or the pornographic literature *sous le manteau*—since serious literature was bound to be idealistic and cautious—which consisted of books of the very worst sort, printed on poor-quality paper, badly written, and yet sure to sell well, like the 'titillating' magazines of a kind no longer available today, or not in such a repulsive and lecherous form. As well as the court theatre, which paid homage to the ideals of the time with its noble sentiments and snow-white purity, there were theatres and cabarets with programmes entirely comprising the smuttiest of dirty jokes. What was suppressed found outlets every-where, found ways around obstacles, ways out of difficulties.

So ultimately the generation that was prudishly denied any sexual enlightenment, any form of easy social encounter with the opposite sex, was a thousand times more erotically obsessed than young people today, who have so much more freedom in love. Forbidden fruit excites a craving, only what is forbidden stimulates desire, and the less the eyes saw and the ears heard the more minds dreamt. The less air, light and sun was allowed to fall on the body, the more heated did the senses become. To sum up, the social pressure put on us as young people, instead of improving our morals, merely made us embittered and distrustful of those in authority. From the first day of our sexual awakening we instinctively felt that this dishonest morality, with its silence and concealment, wanted to take from us something that was rightfully ours in our youth, and was sacrificing our desire for honesty to a convention that had long ago ceased to have any real meaning.

However, the morality of this society, which on the one hand tacitly assumed the existence of sexuality running its natural course, but on the other would not publicly acknowledge it at any price, was in fact doubly mendacious. For while it turned a blind eye to young men and even, winking the other eye, encouraged them to 'sow their wild oats', as the jargon of the time jocularly put it, society closed both eyes in alarm and pretended to be blind when faced with women. Even convention had to admit tacitly that a man felt and must be allowed to feel certain urges. But to admit honestly that a woman was also subject to them, that for its eternal purposes creation required the feminine as well as the masculine principle, would have offended against the whole concept of women as sacred beings. Before Freud, it was an accepted axiom that a woman had no physical desires until they were aroused in her by a man, although of course that was officially permitted only in marriage. However, as the air of Vienna in particular was full of dangerously infectious eroticism even in that age of morality, a girl of good family had to live in an entirely sterilised atmosphere from her birth to the day when she went to the bridal altar. Young girls were not left alone for a moment, for their own protection. Girls had governesses whose duty it was to make sure that they did not—God forbid!—take a step outside the front door of their homes unescorted; they were taken to school, to their dancing classes and music lessons, and then collected again. Every book they read was checked, and above all young girls were kept constantly occupied in case they indulged in any dangerous ideas. They had to practise the piano, do some singing and drawing; they had to learn foreign languages and the history of art and literature; they were educated, indeed over-educated. But while the idea was to make them as educated and socially well brought up as possible, at the same time great care was taken to leave them ignorant of all natural things, in a way unimaginable to us today. A young girl of good family was not allowed to have any idea of how the male body was formed, she must not know how children came into the world, for since she was an angel she was not just to remain physically untouched, she must also enter marriage entirely 'pure' in mind. For a girl to be well brought up at the time was equivalent to leaving her ignorant of life, and that ignorance sometimes remained with women of those days all their lives. I am still amused by the grotesque story of an aunt of mine, who on her wedding night suddenly appeared back in her parents' apartment at one in the morning frantically ringing the bell and protesting that she never wanted to set eyes on the horrible man whom she had married again, he was a madman and a monster! In all seriousness, he had tried to take her clothes off. It was only with difficulty, she said, that she had been able to save herself from his obviously deranged demands.

I cannot deny that, on the other hand, this ignorance lent young girls of the time a mysterious charm. Unfledged as they were, they guessed that besides and beyond their own world there was another of which they knew nothing, were not allowed to know anything, and that made them curious, full of longing, effusive, attractively confused. If you greeted them in the street they would blush—do any young girls still blush? Alone with each other they would giggle and whisper and laugh all the time, as if they were slightly tipsy. Full of expectation of the unknown that was never disclosed to them, they entertained romantic dreams of life, but at the same time were ashamed to think of anyone finding out how much their bodies physically craved a kind of affection of which they had no very clear notion. A sort of slight confusion always animated their conduct. They walked differently from the girls of today, whose bodies are made fit through sport, who mingle with young men easily and without embarrassment, as their equals. Even a thousand paces away in our time, you could tell the difference between a young girl and a woman who had had a physical relationship with a man simply by the way she walked and held herself. Young girls were more girlish than the girls of today, less like women, resembling the exotically tender hothouse plants that are raised in the artificially overheated atmosphere of a glasshouse, away from any breath of inclement wind; the artificially bred product of a certain kind of rearing and culture.

But that was how the society of the time liked its young girls—innocent and ignorant, well brought up and knowing nothing, curious and bashful, uncertain and impractical, destined by an education remote from real life to be formed and guided in marriage by a husband, without any will of their own. Custom and decency seemed to protect them as the emblem of its most secret ideal, the epitome of demure feminine conduct, virginal and unworldly. But what a tragedy if one of these young girls had wasted her time, and at twenty-five or thirty was still unmarried! Convention mercilessly decreed that an unmarried woman of thirty must remain in a state of inexperience and naivety, feeling no desires—it was a state not at all suitable for her at her present age—preserving herself intact for the sake of the family and 'decency'. The tender image of girlhood then usually turned into a sharp and cruel caricature. An unmarried woman of her age had been 'left on the shelf', and a woman left on the shelf became an old maid. The humorous journals, with their shallow mockery, made fun of old maids all the time. If you open old issues of the *Fliegende Blätter* or another specimen of the humorous press of the time, it is horrifying to see, in every edition, the most unfeeling jokes cracked at the expense of aging unmarried women whose nervous systems were so badly disturbed that they could not hide what, after all, was their natural longing for love. Instead of acknowledging the tragedy of these sac-rificial lives which, for the sake of the family and its good name, had to deny the demands of nature and their longing for love and motherhood, people mocked them with a lack of understanding that repels us today. But society is always most cruel to those who betray its secrets, showing where its dishonesty commits a crime against nature.

If bourgeois convention of the time desperately tried to maintain the fiction that a woman of the 'best circles' had no sexuality and must not have any until she was married—for anything else would make her an immoral creature, an outcast from her family—then it was still obliged to admit that such instincts really were present in a young man. And as experience had shown that young men who had reached sexual maturity could not be prevented from putting their sexuality into practice, society limited itself to the modest hope that they could take their unworthy pleasures extramu-rally, outside the sanctified precincts of good manners. Just as cities conceal an underground sewage system into which all the filth of the cesspits is diverted under their neatly swept streets, full of beautiful shops selling luxury goods, beneath their elegant promenades, the entire sexual life of young men was supposed to be conducted out of sight, below the moral surface of society. The dangers to which a young man would expose himself did not matter, or the spheres into which he ventured, and his mentors at school and at home sedulously refrained from explaining anything about that to him. Now and then, in the last years of that moral society's existence, an occasional father with 'enlightened ideas', as it was put at the time, put some thought to the matter and, as soon as the boy began to show signs of growing a beard, tried to help him in a responsible way. He would summon the family doctor; who sometimes asked the young man into a private room, ceremoniously cleaning his glasses before embarking on a lecture about the dangers of sexually transmitted diseases, and urging the young man, who by this time had usually informed himself about them already, to indulge in moderation and remember to take certain precautions. Other fathers employed a still stranger method; they hired a pretty maidservant for their domestic staff, and it was this girl's job to give the young man practical instruction. Such fathers thought it better for a son to get this troublesome business over and done with under their own roof. This method also, to all appearances, preserved decorum and in addition excluded the danger that the young man might fall into the hands of some 'artful and designing person'. *One* method of enlightenment, however, remained firmly banned in all forms and by all those in authority—the open and honest one.

What opportunities were open to a young man of the bourgeois world? In all other classes of society, including the so-called lower classes, the problem was not a problem at all. In the country, a farm labourer of seventeen would be sleeping with a maidservant, and if there were consequences of the relationship it was not so very important. In most of our Alpine villages the numbers of illegitimate children far exceeded those born in wedlock. In the urban proletariat, again, a young working man would 'live in sin' with a woman of his class when he could not afford to get married yet. Among the Orthodox Jews of Galicia, a young man of seventeen who had only just reached sexual maturity was given a bride, and he could be a grandfather by the time he was forty. Only in our bourgeois society was the real solution to the problem, early marriage, frowned upon, because no paterfamilias would have entrusted his daughter to a young man of twenty-two or twenty. Someone so young was not thought mature enough. Here again we can detect dishonesty, for the bourgeois calendar was by no means synchronised with the rhythms of nature. While nature brings a young man to sexual maturity at sixteen or seventeen, in the society of that time he was of marriageable status only when he had a 'position in society', and that was unlikely to be before he was twenty-five or twenty-six. So there was an artificial interval of six, eight or ten years between real sexual maturity and society's idea of it, and in that interval the young man had to fend for himself in his private affairs or 'adventures'.

Not that he was given too many opportunities for them at that time. Only a very few and especially rich young men could afford the luxury of keeping a mistress, meaning renting an apartment for her and providing for her keep. Similarly, a few particularly lucky young men matched a literary ideal of the time in the matter of extramarital love—for extramarital love was the only kind that could be described in novels—and entered into a relationship with a married woman. The rest managed as best they could with shop girls and waitresses, affairs that provided little real satisfaction. Before the emancipation of women, only girls from the very poorest proletarian background had few enough scruples and sufficient liberty to engage in such fleeting relationships when there was no serious prospect of marriage. Poorly dressed, tired out after working at a poorly paid job for twelve hours a day, neglectful of personal hygiene (a bathroom was the privilege of rich families in those days), and reared in a very narrow social class, these poor girls were so far below the intellectual level of their lovers that the young men themselves usually shrank from being seen with them in public. It was true that convention had found a way of dealing with this awkward fact in the institution of *chambres séparées*, as they were known, where you could eat supper with a girl in the evening unobserved, and everything else was done in the small hotels in dark side streets that had been set up exclusively for this trade. But all these encounters were bound to be fleeting and without any real attraction; they were purely sexual rather than erotic, because they were always conducted hastily and surreptitiously, like something forbidden. At best, there was the possibility of a relationship with one of those hybrid beings who were half inside society, half outside it—actresses, dancers, women artists, the only 'emancipated' women of the day. In general, however, the basis of eroticism outside marriage at that time was prostitution, which in a way represented the dark vaulted cellar above which rose the magnificent structure of bourgeois society, with its immaculately dazzling façade.

*

The present generation has little idea of the vast extent of prostitution in Europe before the world wars. While today prostitutes are seen in big cities as seldom as horses in the streets, at the time the pavements were so crowded with women of easy virtue that it was harder to avoid them than to find them. In addition there were all the 'closed houses' or brothels, the night-spots, cabarets and dance halls with their female dancers and singers, the bars with their hostesses. Feminine wares were openly offered for sale at such places, in every price range and at every time of day, and it really cost a man as little time and trouble to hire a woman for quarter-of-an-hour, an hour, or a night as to buy a packet of cigarettes or a newspaper. Nothing seems to me better evidence of the greater and more natural honesty of life and love today than the fact that these days it is possible, and almost taken for granted, for young men to do without this once indispensable institution, and prostitution has been partly eliminated, but not by the efforts of the police or the law. Decreasing demand for this tragic product of pseudo-morality has reduced it to a small remnant.

The official attitude of the state and its morality to these murky affairs was never really comfortable. From the moral standpoint, no one dared to acknowledge a woman's right to sell herself openly; but when hygiene entered the equation it was impossible to do without prostitution, since it provided a channel for the problem of extramarital sexuality. So the authorities resorted to ambiguity by drawing a distinction between unofficial prostitution, which the state opposed as immoral and dangerous, and licensed prostitution, for which a woman needed a kind of certificate and which was taxed by the state. A girl who had made up her mind to become a prostitute got a special licence from the police, and a booklet of her own certifying her profession. By placing herself under police control and dutifully turning up for a medical examination twice a week, she had gained business rights to hire out her body at whatever price she thought appropriate. Her calling was recognised as a profession along with other professions, but all the same—and here came the snag of morality—it was not *fully* recognised. If a prostitute had, for instance, sold her wares, meaning her body, to a man who then refused to pay the agreed price, she could not bring charges against him. At that point her demand had suddenly become an immoral one, and the authorities provided no protection—*ob turpem causam* was the reason given by the law, because it was a dirty trade.

Such details showed up the contradictions in a system that on the one hand gave these women a place in a trade permitted by the state, but on the other considered them personally outcasts beyond the common law. However, the real dishonesty lay in the fact that these restrictions applied only to the poorer classes. A Viennese ballerina who could be bought by any man at any time of day for two hundred crowns, just as a street girl could be bought for two crowns, did not, of course, need a licence; the great *demi-mondaines* even featured in newspaper reports of the prominent spectators present at horse-racing events—trotting races, or the Derby—because they themselves belonged to 'society'. In the same way, some of the most distinguished procuresses, women who supplied the court, the aristocracy and the rich bourgeoisie with luxury goods, were outside the law, which otherwise imposed severe prison sentences for procuring. Strict discipline, merciless supervision and social ostracism applied only to the army of thousands upon thousands of prostitutes whose bodies and humiliated souls were recruited to defend an ancient and long-since-eroded concept of morality against free, natural forms of love.

This monstrous army of prostitutes was divided into different kinds, just as the real army was divided into cavalry, artillery, infantry and siege artillery. In prostitution, the closest equivalent to the siege artillery was the group that adopted certain streets of the city as their own quarter. These were usually areas where, during the Middle Ages, the gallows, a leper house or a graveyard used to stand, places frequented by outlaws, hangmen and other social outcasts. The better class of citizens had preferred to avoid such parts of the city for centuries, and the authorities allowed a few alleys there to be used as a market for love. Two hundred or five hundred women would sit next door to one another, side by side, on display at the windows of their single-storey apartments, as twentieth-century prostitutes still do in Yoshiwara in Japan or the Cairo fish market. They were cheap goods working in shifts, a day shift and a night shift.

Itinerant prostitutes corresponded to the cavalry or infantry; these were the countless girls for sale trying to pick up customers in the street. Street-walkers of this kind were said in Vienna to be *auf den Strich*,[4] because the police had divided up the street with invisible lines, leaving the girls their own patches in which to advertise. Dressed in a tawdry elegance which they had gone to great pains to purchase, they paraded around the streets day and night, until well into the hours of dawn, even in freezing and wet weather, constantly forcing their weary and badly painted faces into an enticing smile for every passer-by. All the big cities today look to me more beautiful and humane places now that these crowds of hungry, unhappy women no longer populate the streets, offering pleasure for sale without any expectation of pleasure themselves, and in their endless wanderings from place to place, all finally going the same inevitable way—to the hospital.

But even these throngs of women were not enough to satisfy the constant demand. Some men preferred to indulge themselves more discreetly and in greater comfort than by picking up these sad, fluttering nocturnal birds of paradise in the street. They wanted a more agreeable kind of lovemaking in the light and warmth, with music and dancing and a pretence of luxury. For these clients there were the 'closed houses', the brothels. The girls gathered there in a so-called salon furnished with fake luxury, some of them in ladylike outfits, some already unequivocally clad in negligees. A pianist provided musical entertainment, there was drinking and dancing and light conversation before the couples discreetly withdrew to bedrooms. In many of the more elegant houses, brothels that had a certain international fame (to be found particularly in Paris and Milan), a naive mind could imagine that he had been invited to a private house with some rather high-spirited society ladies. In addition, the girls in these houses were better off than the street-walkers. They did not have to walk through the dirt of alleyways in wind and rain; they sat in a warm room, had good clothes, plenty to eat and in particular plenty to drink. In reality, however, they were prisoners of their madams, who forced them to buy the clothes they wore at extortionate prices, and played such arithmetical tricks with the expense of their board and lodging that even a girl who worked with great industry and stamina was always in debt to the madam in some way, and could never leave the house of her own free will.

It would be intriguing, and good documentary evidence of the culture of that time, to write the secret history of many of these houses, for they held the most remarkable secrets, which of course were well known to the otherwise stern authorities. There were secret doors, and special staircases up which members of the very highest society—even, it was rumoured, gentlemen from the court—could visit these places, unseen by other mortals. There were rooms lined with mirrors, and others offering secret views of the rooms next door, where couples engaged in sex unaware that they were being watched. There were all kinds of strange costumes for the girls to wear, from nuns' habits to ballerinas' tutus, kept in drawers and chests ready for men with special fetishes. And this was the same city, the same society, the same morality that expressed horror if young girls rode bicycles, and called it a violation of the dignity of science for Freud, in his clear, calm and cogent manner, to state certain truths that they did not like to acknowledge. The same world that so emotionally defended the purity of woman tolerated this horrifying trade in female bodies, organised it and even profited by it.

*

So we must not be misled by the sentimental novels and novellas of that period; it was not a good time for the young when girls were placed in airtight compartments under the control of their families, sealed off from life, their physical and intellectual development stunted, and when young men in turn were forced into secrecy and underhand behaviour, all in support of a morality that at heart no one believed in or obeyed. Straightforward, honest relationships, exactly what ought to have been bringing happiness and delight to these young people by the laws of nature, were granted to only very few. And any man of that generation trying to be honest in recollecting his very first encounters with women will find few episodes on which he can really look back with unclouded pleasure. For apart from the social constraints always urging young men to be cautious and preserve secrecy, there was another element at the time to cast a shadow on their minds, even at the most intimate moments—the fear of infection. Here again the young men of the time were at a particular disadvantage compared to those of today, for it must not be forgotten that forty years ago sexual diseases were a hundred times more prevalent than they are now, and above all a hundred times more dangerous and terrible in their effects, because clinical practice did not yet know how to deal with them. There was still no scientific possibility of curing them as quickly and radically as today, when they are little more than a passing episode. While thanks to the treatment developed by Paul Ehrlich,[5] weeks may now pass at the teaching hospitals of small and medium-sized universities without a professor's being able to show his students a new case of syphilis, statistics of that time showed that in the army, and in big cities, at least one or two in every ten young men had already contracted an infection. Young people at the time were constantly warned of the danger; walking through the streets of Vienna, you could read a plate on every sixth or seventh building proclaiming that a 'specialist in skin and venereal diseases' practised there, and to the fear of infection was added horror at the repellent, degrading nature of treatment at the time. Again, today's world knows nothing of that. The entire body of a man infected with syphilis was subjected to weeks and weeks of treatment by rubbing with quicksilver, which made the teeth fall out and caused other kinds of damage to the patient's health. The unfortunate victim of a bad attack felt not only mentally but also physically soiled, and even after such a terrible cure he could never for the rest of his life be sure that the malicious virus might not wake from its dormancy at any moment, paralysing him from the spinal marrow outwards and softening the brain inside his skull. No wonder that at the time many young men diagnosed with the disease immediately reached for a revolver, finding it intolerable to feel hopelessly suspect to themselves and their close family. Then there were the other anxieties resulting from a *vita sexualis* pursued only in secrecy. If I try to remember truthfully, I know hardly one of the comrades of my adolescent years who did not at some time look pale and distracted—one because he was sick or feared he would fall sick, another because he was being blackmailed over an abortion, a third because he lacked the money to take a course of treatment without his family's knowledge, a fourth because he didn't know how to pay the alimony for a child claimed by a waitress to be his, a fifth because his wallet had been stolen in a brothel and he dared not go to the police. So youth in that pseudo-moral age was much more dramatic and on the other hand unclean, much more exciting and at the same time oppressive, than the novels and plays of the court writers describe it. In the sphere of Eros, young people were almost never allowed the freedom and happiness proper to them at their time of life, any more than they were permitted it at school and at home.

All this has to be emphasised in an honest portrait of the time, because in talking to younger friends of the post-war generation, I often find it very hard to convince them that our young days were definitely not to be preferred to theirs. Certainly, we had more freedom as citizens of the state than the present generation, who are obliged to do military service or labour service, or in many countries to embrace a mass ideology, and are indeed generally at the mercy of the arbitrary stupidity of international politics. We could devote ourselves undisturbed to our artistic and intellectual inclinations; we could pursue our private lives in a more individual and personal way. We were able to live in a more cosmopolitan manner; the whole world was open to us. We could travel anywhere we liked without passes and permits; no one interrogated us about our beliefs, our origins, our race or religion. We certainly did—I do not deny it—have immeasurably more individual freedom, and we did not just welcome that, we made use of it. But as Friedrich Hebbel once nicely put it, "Sometimes we have no wine, sometimes we have no goblet." Both are seldom granted to one and the same generation; if morality allows a man freedom, the state tries to remould him. If the state allows him freedom, morality will try to impose itself. We knew more of the world then, and knew it better, but the young today live their own youthful years more fully and are more aware of what they experience. Today, when I see young people coming out of their schools and colleges with heads held high, with bright, cheerful faces, when I see boys and girls together in free and easy companionship, competing with each other in studies, sport and games without false shame or bashfulness, racing over the snow on skis, rivalling each other in the swimming pool with the freedom known in the ancient world, driving over the countryside together in motor cars, engaging in all aspects of a healthy, untroubled life like brothers and sisters, without any internal or external pressure on them, I always feel as if not forty but a thousand years lay between them and those of us who had to look for any experience of giving and taking love in a hole-and-corner way in the shadows. I see genuinely happy expressions on their faces. What a great revolution in morality has taken place to the benefit of the young; how much freedom in life and love they have regained, and how much better they thrive both physically and mentally on this healthy new freedom! Women look more beautiful to me now that they are at liberty to display their figures; their gait is more upright, their eyes brighter, their conversation less stilted. What a different kind of confidence this new youth has acquired! They are not called upon by anyone else to account for what they do or do not do—they answer only to themselves and their own sense of responsibility, which has wrested control over them from mothers and fathers and aunts and teachers, and long ago threw off the inhibition, intimidation and tension that weighed down on their own development. They no longer know the devious secrecy we had to resort to to get the forbidden pleasures that they now correctly feel are their right. They happily enjoy their youth with the verve, freshness, lightness of heart and freedom from anxiety proper to their age. But the best of that happiness, it seems to me, is that they do not have to lie to others, while they can be honest with themselves and their natural feelings and desires. It is possible that the carefree way in which young people go through life today means they lack something of our own veneration for intellectual subjects when we were young. It may be that through the easy give and take that is accepted now, they lose an aspect of love that seemed to us particularly valuable and intriguing, they lose a certain reticence caused by shame and timidity, and certain especially tender moments. Perhaps they do not even have any idea how the awe of what is banned and forbidden mysteriously enhances one's enjoyment of it. But all this seems to me a minor drawback by comparison with the saving grace—the fact that young people today are free from fear and oppression, and enjoy in full what was forbidden us at their age, a sense of frank self-confidence.

NOTES

1 *What is natural is vile.*

2 *La Dame aux camélias,* novel by Alexandre Dumas *fils*, on which Verdi's famous opera *La Traviata* is based.

3 Bjørnstjerne Bjørnson, 1832-1910, Norwegian novelist who won the Nobel Prize for Literature in 1903.

4 *Strich*—line or break. To be *auf den Strich* has gone into the German language as an expression for street-walking or being on the game.

5 Paul Ehrlich, 1854-1915, distinguished German immunologist who won the Nobel Prize for Medicine in 1908.

UNIVERSITAS VITAE

A T LAST THE LONG-AWAITED moment came, and with the last year of the old century we could also close the door of the hated grammar school behind us. After we had passed our final school examinations, not altogether easily— what did we know about mathematics, physics, and the rest of the scholastic curriculum?—the school principal honoured us with a valedictory speech, delivered with great feeling, an occasion for which we had to wear black frock coats. We were now grown up, he said, and our industry and efficiency must do credit to our native land. Eight years of companionship thus came to an end, and I have seen very few of my comrades in adversity since then. Most of us registered at the university, and those who had to reconcile themselves to other careers and occupations regarded us with envy.

For in those long-distant days in Austria there was still a special, romantic aura about university. The status of a student brought with it certain privileges that gave a young scholar a great advantage over all his contemporaries. I doubt whether much is known outside the German-speaking countries about the old-fashioned oddity of this phenomenon, so its anachronistic absurdity calls for explanation. Most of our universities had been founded in the Middle Ages, at a time when occupying your mind with academic knowledge appeared out of the ordinary, and young men were given certain privileges to induce them to study. Medieval scholars were not subject to the ordinary civil courts, they could not have writs served on them or be otherwise pestered by bailiffs in their colleges, they wore special clothing, had a right to fight duels with impunity, and were recognised as an exclusive guild with its own traditions—be they good or bad. In the course of time, with the gradual coming of democracy to public life and the dissolution of all other medieval guilds, academics in the rest of Europe lost this privileged position. Only in Germany and German-speaking Austria, where class consciousness still had the upper hand, did students cling tenaciously to privileges which had long ago lost any meaning. They even based their own student code of conduct on them. A German student set particular store by a specific kind of 'student honour', existing side by side with his honour as an ordinary citizen. Anyone who insulted him must give him satisfaction, meaning that if the man offering the insult was 'fit to give satisfaction' they must fight a duel. This smug student criterion of 'fitness to give satisfaction', in turn, could not be met by someone like a businessman or a banker, only a man with an academic education, a graduate, or a military officer—no one else, among millions, was good enough to have the honour of crossing swords with one of those stupid, beardless boys. Then again, to be considered a real student you had to have proved your courage, meaning you had fought as many duels as possible, and even showed the signs of those heroic deeds on your face in the form of duelling scars; unscarred cheeks and a nose without a nick in it were unworthy of an academic in the genuine German tradition. This meant that the students who wore fraternity colours, showing that they belonged to a particular student body, felt obliged to go in for mutual provocation, also insulting other perfectly peaceful students and officers so that they could fight more duels. In the fraternities, every new student had his aptitude for this worthy occupation tested on the fencing floor, and he was also initiated into other fraternity customs. Every 'fox', the term for a novice, was assigned to an older fraternity member whom he had to serve with slavish obedience, and who in turn instructed him in the noble arts required by the student code of conduct, which amounted to drinking until you threw up. The acid test was to empty a heavy tankard of beer in a single draught, proving in this glorious manner that you were no weakling, or to bawl student songs in chorus and defy the police by going on the rampage and goose-stepping through the streets by night. All this was considered manly, proper student behaviour, suitably German, and when the fraternities went out on a Saturday, waving their banners and wearing their colourful caps and ribbons, these simple-minded young men, with senseless arrogance fostered by their own activities, felt that they were the true representatives of intellectual youth. They looked down with contempt on the common herd who did not know enough to pay proper tribute to this academic culture of German manliness.

To a boy still wet behind the ears, coming to Vienna straight from a provincial grammar school, such dashing, merry student days may well have seemed the epitome of all that was romantic. For decades to come, indeed, when village notaries and physicians now getting on in years were in their cups, they would look up with much emotion at the crossed swords and colourful student ribbons hanging on the walls of their rooms, and proudly bore their duelling scars as the marks of their 'academic' status. To us, however, this stupid, brutish way of life was nothing short of abhorrent, and if we met a member of those beribboned hordes we sensibly kept out of his way. We saw individual freedom as the greatest good, and to us this urge for aggression, combined with a tendency towards servility en masse, was only too clearly evidence of the worst and most dangerous aspects of the German mind. We also knew that this artificially mummified romanticism hid some very cleverly calculated and practical aims, for membership of a duelling fraternity ensured a young man the patronage of its former members who now held high office, and would smooth the path for his subsequent career. Joining the Borussia fraternity in Bonn was the one sure way into the German Diplomatic Service; membership of the Catholic fraternities in Austria led to well-endowed benefices in the gift of the ruling Catholic Socialist party, and most of these 'heroes' knew very well that in future their coloured student ribbons would have to make up for the serious studies they had neglected, and that a couple of duelling scars on their faces could be much more useful in a job application than anything they had inside their heads. The mere sight of those uncouth, militarised gangs, those scarred and boldly provocative faces, spoilt my visits to the university halls, and when other students who genuinely wanted to study went to the university library they, too, avoided going through the main hall, opting for an inconspicuous back door so as not to meet these pathetic heroes.

It had been decided long ago by my family, consulting together, that I was to study at the university. The only question was which faculty to choose. My parents left that entirely to me. My elder brother had already joined our father's business, so for me, as the second son, there was no great hurry. After all, it was just a case of making sure, for the sake of the family honour, that I gained a doctorate, never mind in what subject. Curiously enough, I didn't mind what subject either. I had long ago given my heart to literature, so none of the professionally taught academic branches of knowledge really interested me in themselves. I even had a secret distrust, which has not yet left me, of all academic pursuits. Emerson's axiom that good books are a substitute for the best university still seems to me accurate, and I am convinced to this day that one can become an excellent philosopher, historian, literary philologist, lawyer, or anything else without ever having gone to university or even a grammar school. In ordinary everyday life I have found confirmation, again and again, that in practice second-hand booksellers often know more about books than the professors who lecture on them; art dealers know more than academic art historians; and many of the most important ideas and discoveries in all fields come from outsiders. Practical, useful and salutary as academic life may be for those of average talent, it seems to me that creative individuals can dispense with it, and may even be inhibited by the academic approach, in particular at a university like ours in Vienna. It had six or seven thousand students, whose potentially fruitful personal contact with their teachers was restricted from the first by overcrowding, and it had fallen behind the times because of excessive loyalty to its traditions. I did not meet a single man there whose knowledge would have held me spellbound. So the real criterion of my choice was not what subject most appealed to me in itself, but which would burden me least and would allow me the maximum time and liberty for my real passion. I finally chose philosophy—or rather, 'exact philosophy', as the old curriculum called it in our time—but not out of any real sense of a vocation, since I do not have much aptitude for purely abstract thought. Without exception, my ideas come to me from objects, events and people, and everything purely theoretical and metaphysical remains beyond my grasp. But in exact philosophy the purely abstract material to be mastered was well within bounds, and it would be easy to avoid attending lectures and classes. I would only have to hand in a dissertation at the end of my eighth semester and take a few exams. So I drew up a plan for my time—for three years I would not bother with my university studies at all. Then, in my final year, I would put on a strenuous spurt, master the academic material and dash off some kind of dissertation. The university would thus have given me all I really wanted of it: a couple of years of freedom to lead my own life and concentrate on my artistic endeavours—*universitas vitae*, the university of life.

When I look back at my life I can remember few happier moments than those at the beginning of what might be called my non-university studies. I was young, and did not yet feel that I ought to be achieving perfection. I was reasonably independent, the day had twenty-four hours in it and they were all mine. I could read what I liked and work on what I liked, without having to account to anyone for it. The cloud of academic exams did not yet loom on the bright horizon. To a nineteen-year-old, three years are a long time, rich and ample in its possibilities, full of potential surprises and gifts!

The first thing I began to do was to make a collection—an unsparing selection, as I thought—of my own poems. I am not ashamed to confess that at nineteen, fresh from grammar school, printer's ink seemed to me the finest smell on earth, sweeter than attar of roses from Shiraz. Whenever I had a poem accepted for publication in a newspaper, my self-confidence, not naturally very strong, was boosted. Shouldn't I take the crucial step of trying to get a whole volume published? The encouragement of my friends, who believed in me more than I believed in myself, made up my mind for me. I was bold enough to submit the manuscript to the most outstanding publishing house of the time specialising in German poetry, Schuster & Löffler, the publishers of Liliencron, Dehmel, Bierbaum and Mombert,[1] in fact the whole generation of poets who, with Rilke and Hofmannsthal at the same period, had created the new German style. And then, marvellous to relate, along in quick succession came those unforgettably happy moments, never to be repeated in a writer's life even after his greatest successes. A letter arrived with the publisher's colophon on it. I held it uneasily in my hands, hardly daring to open it. Next came the moment, when, with bated breath, I read the news it contained—the firm had decided to publish my poems, and even wanted an option on my next one as a condition. After that came a package with the first proofs, which I undid with the greatest excitement to see the typeface, the design of the page, the embryonic form of the book, and then, a few weeks later, the book itself, the first copies. I never tired of looking at them, feeling them, comparing them with each other again and again and again. Then there was the childish impulse to visit bookshops and see if they had copies on display, and if so whether those copies were in the middle of the shop, or lurking inconspicuously in some corner. After that came the wait for letters, for the first reviews, for the first communication from unknown and unpredictable quarters—such suspense and excitement, such moments of enthusiasm! I secretly envy young people offering their first books to the world those moments. But this delight of mine was not self-satisfaction; it was only a case of love at first sight. Anyone can work out, from the mere fact that I have never allowed these *Silberne Saiten*—Silver Strings—the title of my now forgotten firstborn, to be reprinted, what I myself soon came to feel about those early verses. Nor did I not let a single one of them appear in my collected poetry. They were verses of vague premonition and unconscious empathy, arising not from my own experience but from a passion for language. They did show a certain musicality and enough sense of form to get them noticed in interested circles, and I could not complain of any lack of encouragement. Liliencron and Dehmel, the leading poets of the time, gave warm and even comradely recognition, to their nineteen-year-old author; Rilke, whom I idolised, sent me, in return for my "attractively produced book" a copy from a special edition of his latest poems inscribed to me "with thanks". I saved this work from the ruins of Austria as one of the finest mementos of my youth, and brought it to England. (I wonder where it is today?) At the end, it seemed to me almost eerie that this kind present to me from Rilke—the first of many—was now forty years old, and his familiar handwriting greeted me from the domain of the dead. But the most unexpected surprise of all was that Max Reger, together with Richard Strauss the greatest living composer, asked my permission to set six poems from this volume to music. I have often heard one or another of them at concerts since then—my own verses, long forgotten and dismissed from my own mind, but brought back over the intervening time by the fraternal art of a master.

This unhoped-for approval, together with a friendly reception by the critics, encouraged me to take a step that, in my incurable self-distrust, I would never otherwise have taken, or not so early. Even when I was at school I had published short novellas and essays as well as poems in the modern literary journals, but I had never tried offering any of these works to a powerful newspaper with a wide circulation. There was really only one such quality newspaper in Vienna, the *Neue Freie Presse*, which with its high-minded stance, its concentration on culture and its political prestige occupied much the same position thoughout the entire Austro-Hungarian Monarchy as *The Times* did in England and *Le Temps* in France. None of even the imperial German newspapers were so intent on maintaining a high cultural level. The editor, Moritz Benedikt, a man of inexhaustible industry and with a phenomenal talent for organisation, put all his positively daemonic energy into outshining all the German newspapers in the fields of literature and culture. When he wanted something from a famous author, no expense was spared; ten, twenty telegrams were sent off to him one after another, any kind of fee agreed in advance; the literary supplements of the holiday numbers at Christmas and New Year were whole volumes full of the greatest names of the time. Anatole France, Gerhart Hauptmann, Ibsen, Zola, Strindberg and Shaw found themselves keeping company in the paper on such occasions, and its influence on the literary orientation of the entire city and country was immeasurable. Progressive and liberal in its views as a matter of course, sound and circumspect in its opinions, this paper was a fine example of the high cultural standards of old Austria.

There was a special holy of holies in this temple of progress, the section known as the 'feuilleton' which, like the great daily papers of Paris, *Le Temps* and *Le Journal des Débats*, published the best and soundest essays on poetry, the theatre, music and art under a line at the bottom of the page, keeping it clearly distinct from the ephemera of politics and the news of the day. Only authorities who had proved their worth could write for this section. Nothing but sound judgement, wide experience over many years and perfect artistic form could get an author who had proved himself over the course of time into this sanctuary. Ludwig Speidel, a master essayist, and Eduard Hanslick had the same papal authority in the fields of the theatre and music as Sainte-Beuve in his columns known as *les Lundis* in Paris. The thumbs-up or thumbs-down of these critics determined the success in Vienna of a musical work, a play, a book, and often of its author or composer himself. At the time every one of these feuilleton essays was the talk of the town in educated circles; they were discussed and criticised, they aroused admiration or hostility, and when now and then a new writer's name appeared among the long-acknowledged feuilletonists, it created a sensation. Of the younger generation, only Hofmannsthal had sometimes found his way into the feuilleton with some of his best essays; other young authors had to be satisfied if they could contrive to get themselves into the separate literary supplement of the paper. As Vienna saw it, an author writing in the feuilleton on the front page had his name carved in marble.

How I found the courage to submit a small essay on poetry to the *Neue Freie Presse*, which my father regarded as an oracle and the abode of the Lord's anointed, is more than I can understand today. But after all, nothing worse than rejection could happen to me. The editor of the feuilleton interviewed would-be essayists only once a week, between two and three o'clock, since the regular cycle of famous and firmly established contributors very seldom left any room for an outsider's work. With my heart racing, I climbed the little spiral staircase to his office and sent in my name. A few minutes later the servant came back—the editor of the feuilleton would see me, and I entered the small, cramped room.

The editor of the feuilleton of the *Neue Freie Presse* was Theodor Herzl, and he was the first man of international stature whom I had met in my life—not that I knew what great changes he would bring to the destiny of the Jewish people and the

THE SOCIETY OF THE CROSSED KEYS

history of our times. His position at that point was rather contradictory and indeterminate. He had set out to become a writer, had shown dazzling journalistic talents at an early age, and became the darling of the Viennese public first as Paris correspondent of the *Neue Freie Presse*, then as a writer for its feuilleton. His essays are still captivating in their wealth of sharp and often wise observation, their felicity of style and their high-minded tone, which never lost its natural distinction even when he was in cheerful or critical mood. They were the most cultivated imaginable kind of journalism, and delighted a city that had trained itself to appreciate subtlety. He had also had a play successfully produced at the Burgtheater, and now he was a highly esteemed man, idolised by us young people and respected by our fathers, until one day the unexpected happened. Fate can always find a way to track down the man it needs for its secret purposes, even if he tries to hide from it.

Theodor Herzl had had an experience in Paris that shook him badly, one of those moments that change an entire life. As Paris correspondent, he had been present at the official degradation of Alfred Dreyfus. He had seen the epaulettes torn from the pale man's uniform as he cried out aloud, "I am innocent." And he had known in his heart at that moment that Dreyfus was indeed innocent, and only the fact that he was Jewish had brought the terrible suspicion of treason down on him. As a student, Theodor Herzl had already suffered in his straightforward and manly pride from the fate of the Jews—or rather, thanks to his prophetic insight, he had anticipated all its tragic significance at a time when it hardly seemed a serious matter. At that time, with a sense of being a

born leader, which was justified by both his extremely imposing physical appearance and the wide scope of his mind and
his knowledge of the world, he had formed the fantastic plan
of bringing the Jewish problem to an end once and for all
by uniting Jews and Christians in voluntary mass-baptism.
Always inclined to think in dramatic terms, he had imagined
himself leading thousands upon thousands of Austrian Jews
in a long procession to St Stephen's Cathedral, there to liberate his persecuted, homeless people for ever from the curse
of segregation and hatred in an exemplary symbolic act. He
had soon realised that this plan was impracticable, and years
of his own work had distracted him from the problem at the
heart of his life, although he saw solving it as his true vocation.
However, at the moment when he saw Dreyfus degraded the
idea of his own people's eternal ostracism went to his heart
like a dagger. If segregation is inevitable, he said to himself,
why not make it complete? If humiliation is always to be our
fate, let us meet it with pride. If we suffer from the lack of a
home, let us build ourselves one! So he published his pamphlet
on *The Jewish State*, in which he pronounced all adaptation
through assimilation and all hope of total tolerance impossible
for the Jewish people. They would have to found a new home
for themselves in their old homeland of Palestine.

When this pamphlet, which was short but had the power and
forcefulness of a steel bolt, was published I was still at school,
but I remember the general astonishment and annoyance it
aroused in bourgeois Jewish circles in Vienna. What on earth,
they said angrily, has that usually clever, witty and cultivated
writer Herzl taken into his head? What stupid stuff is he saying

and writing? Why would we want to go to Palestine? We speak German, not Hebrew, our home is in beautiful Austria. Aren't we very well off under good Emperor Franz Joseph? Don't we make a respectable living and enjoy a secure position? Don't we have equal rights, aren't we loyal, established citizens of our beloved Vienna? And don't we live in a progressive time which will do away with all religious prejudice within a few decades? If he's a Jew who wants to help other Jews, why does he present our worst enemies with arguments, trying to segregate us from the German-speaking world when every day unites us more closely with it? Rabbis waxed indignant in their pulpits, the managing director of the *Neue Freie Presse* banned even the mention of the word Zionism in his allegedly progressive newspaper. Karl Kraus, the Thersites of Viennese literature and a past master of venomous mockery, wrote a pamphlet entitled *A Crown for Zion*, and when Theodor Herzl entered the theatre sarcastic murmurs ran through the rows of spectators: "Here comes His Majesty!"

At first Herzl could reasonably feel misunderstood—Vienna, where he thought himself most secure after enjoying years of popularity, was abandoning him, even laughing at him. But then the answer came thundering back with such a weight of approval that he was almost alarmed to see what a mighty movement, far greater than his own person, he had called into being with his few dozen pages. Admittedly the answer did not come from the well-situated, middle-class Western Jews with their comfortable lives, but from the great masses in the East, the Galician, Polish and Russian proletariat. Without knowing it, Herzl's pamphlet had fanned the heart of Judaism into flame. The Messianic dream, two thousand years old, of the return to the Promised Land as affirmed in the holy books, had been smouldering among the ashes of foreign domination. It was a hope and at the same time a religious certainty, the one thing that still gave meaning to life for those downtrodden and oppressed millions. Whenever someone, whether prophet or impostor, had plucked that string in the millennia of exile, the soul of the people had vibrated in sympathy, but never so powerfully as now, never echoing back with such a clamorous roar. One man, with a few dozen pages, had shaped a scattered and disunited throng into a single entity.

That first moment, when the idea was still taking dreamlike but uncertain shape, was to be the happiest in Herzl's short life. As soon as he began to define the aims of the movement in real terms, trying to combine its forces, he could not help seeing how different these people had become under various different nationalities, with their different histories, sometimes religious, sometimes free-thinking, some of them socialist and others capitalist Jews, stirring themselves up against each other in a wide variety of languages, and none of them willing to fall into line with a single unified authority. In the year 1901, when I first met him, he was in mid-struggle, and was perhaps at odds with himself as well; he did not yet believe in ultimate success enough to give up the post that earned him and his family a living. He had to divide himself between his lesser work of journalism and the mission that was his real life. It was as feuilleton editor that Theodor Herzl received me that day.

*

Theodor Herzl rose to greet me, and instinctively I felt there was a grain of truth in the ill-intentioned joke about the King of Zion—he really did look regal with his high forehead, his clear-cut features, his long and almost blue-black beard and his deep-blue, melancholy eyes. His sweeping, rather theatrical gestures did not seem affected, because they arose from a natural dignity, and it would not have taken this particular occasion to make him look imposing to me. Even standing in front of the shabby desk heaped high with papers in that miserably cramped editorial office with its single window, he was like a Bedouin desert sheikh; a billowing white burnous would have looked as natural on him as his black morning coat, well-cut in an obviously Parisian style. After a brief and deliberately inserted pause—as I often noticed later, he liked such small effects, and had probably studied them at the Burgtheater—he deigned to give me his hand, though in a very friendly way. Indicating the chair beside him, he asked, "I think I've heard or read your name somewhere before. You write poetry, don't you?" I said that I did. "Well," he said leaning back, "so what have you brought me?"

I told him I would very much like to submit a little prose essay to him, and handed him my manuscript. He looked at the title page, turned to the end to assess its extent, and then leant back further in his chair. And to my surprise (I had not expected it) I saw that he had already begun to read the manuscript. He read slowly, turning the page without looking up. When he had finished the final page, he slowly folded the manuscript, then ceremoniously and still without looking at me put it into an envelope, and wrote something on the envelope in pencil. Only then, after keeping me in suspense for some time with these mysterious moves, did he raise his dark, weighty glance to me, saying with deliberate and slow solemnity, "I am glad to tell you that your fine piece is accepted for publication in the feuilleton of the *Neue Freie Presse*." It was like Napoleon presenting a young sergeant with the cross of the Légion d'Honneur on the battlefield.

This may seem a minor, unimportant episode in itself. But you would have to be Viennese, and Viennese of my generation, to understand what a meteoric rise this encouragement meant. In my nineteenth year, I had risen to a position of prominence overnight, and Theodor Herzl, who was kind to me from that first moment, used the occasion of our meeting to say, in one of his next essays, that no one should believe the arts were in decline in Vienna. On the contrary, he wrote, as well as Hofmannsthal there were now a number of gifted young writers around who might be expected to do great things, and he mentioned my name first. I have always felt it a particular distinction that a man of the towering importance of Theodor Herzl, in his highly visible and thus very responsible position, was the first to express support for me.

It was a difficult decision for me to make when I said later, with apparent ingratitude, that I felt I could not join his Zionist movement actively and even help him to lead it, as he had asked. However, I could never have made a real success of such a connection; I was alienated most of all by the lack of respect, hardly imaginable today, that his real comrades expressed towards Herzl himself. The Eastern Jews complained that he understood nothing about the Jewish way of life and wasn't even conversant with Jewish customs, while the economists among them regarded him as a mere journalist and feuilletonist. Everyone had his own objection, and did not always express it respectfully. I knew how much goodwill, particularly just then, those truly attuned to Herz's ideas, particularly the young, could and should owe him, and the quarrelsome, opinionated spirit of constant opposition, the lack of honest, heartfelt acceptance in the Zionist circle, estranged me from a movement that I would willingly have approached with curiosity, if only for Herzl's sake. Once, when we were discussing the subject, I openly confessed my dislike of the indiscipline in his ranks. He smiled rather bitterly and said, "Don't forget, we've been used to dealing with problems and arguing over ideas for centuries. After all, historically speaking, we Jews have gone two thousand years without any experience of bringing something real into the world. Unconditional commitment has to be learnt, and I still haven't learnt it myself. I still write for feuilletons now and then, I am still Feuilleton Editor of the *Neue Freie Presse*, when it should really be my duty to have only one thought in the world and never write a line about anything else. But I'm on my way to rectifying that; I'll have to learn unconditional commitment myself first, and then maybe the rest of them will learn with me." I still remember the deep impression these remarks made on me, for none of us could understand why it took Herzl so long to give up his position with the *Neue Freie Presse*—we thought it was for his family's sake. But the world did not know until much later that such was not the case, and he had even sacrificed his own private fortune to the cause. This conversation showed me how much Herzl suffered personally in this dilemma, and many accounts in his diaries confirm it.

I met him many more times, but of all our encounters only one other seems to me really worth remembering, indeed unforgettable, because it was the last. I had been abroad, keeping in touch with Vienna only by letter, and met him one day in the city park. He was obviously coming away from the editorial offices, walking very slowly and not with his old, swinging step, but stooping slightly. I greeted him politely and was going to pass on, but he quickly came towards me, straightening his posture, and gave me his hand. "Now, why are you hiding away? There's no need for that." He approved of my frequent trips abroad. "It's our only way," he said. "All I know I learnt abroad. Only there do you get used to thinking on a wide scale. I'm sure that I would never have had the courage to form my first concept here, it would have been nipped in the bud. But thank God, when I came up with it, it was all ready, and they couldn't do anything but try tripping me up." He then spoke very bitterly about Vienna where, he said, he had found most opposition, and if new initiatives had not come from outside, particularly from the East and now from America too, he would have grown weary. "What's more," he said, "my mistake was to begin too late. Victor Adler was leader of the Social Democratic party at the age of thirty, the age when he was best fitted for the struggle, and I won't even speak of the great figures of history. If you knew how I suffer mentally, thinking of the lost years—regretting that I didn't find my vocation earlier. If my health were as strong as my will, then all would still be well, but you can't buy back the past." I went back to his house with him. Arriving there, he stopped, shook hands with me, and said, "Why do you never come to see me? You've never visited me at home. Telephone first and I'll make sure I am free." I promised him, firmly determined not to keep that promise, for the more I love someone the more I respect his time.

But I did join him after all, only a few months later. The illness that was beginning to make him stoop at that last meeting of ours had suddenly felled him, and now I could accompany him only to the cemetery. It was a strange day, a day in July, and no one who was there will ever forget it. For suddenly people arrived at all the Viennese railway stations, coming with every train by day and night, from all lands and countries; Western, Eastern, Russian, Turkish Jews—from all the provinces and small towns they suddenly stormed in, the shock of the news of his death still showing on their faces. You never felt more clearly what their quarrels and talking had veiled over—the leader of a great movement was being carried to his grave. It was an endless procession. Suddenly Vienna realised that it was not only a writer, an author of moderate importance, who had died, but one of those original thinkers who rise victorious in a country and among its people only at rare intervals. There was uproar in the cemetery itself; too many mourners suddenly poured like a torrent up to his coffin, weeping, howling and screaming in a wild explosion of despair. There was an almost raging turmoil; all order failed in the face of a kind of elemental, ecstatic grief. I have never seen anything like it at a funeral before or since. And I could tell for the first time from all this pain, rising in sudden great outbursts from the hearts of a crowd a million strong, how much passion and hope this one lonely man had brought into the world by the force of his ideas.

The real significance to me of my ceremonial admission to the rank of feuilletonist on the *Neue Freie Presse* was in my private life. It gave me unexpected confidence within the family. My parents had little to do with literature, and did not presume to make literary judgements; to them, and to the entire Viennese bourgeoisie, important works were those that won praise in the *Neue Freie Presse*, and works ignored or condemned there didn't matter. They felt that anything published in the feuilleton was vouched for by the highest authority, and a writer who pronounced judgement there demanded respect merely by virtue of that fact. And now, imagine such a family glancing daily at the front page of their newspaper with reverent awe and one morning, incredibly, finding that the rather unkempt nineteen-year-old sitting at their table, who had been far from a high-flyer at school and whose writing they accepted with kindly tolerance as a harmless diversion (better than playing cards or flirting with disreputable girls, anyway), has been giving his opinions, not much valued previously at home, in that highly responsible journal among famous and experienced men. If I had written the finest poems of Keats, Hölderlin or Shelley, it would not have caused such a total change of attitude in my entire family circle. When I came into the theatre, they pointed this puzzling Benjamin of theirs out to each other, a lad who in some mysterious way had entered the sacred precincts of the old and dignified. And since I was published quite often in the feuilleton, almost on a regular basis, I soon risked winning high esteem and respect locally. But fortunately I avoided that danger in good time by telling my parents one morning, to their surprise, that I would like to spend the next semester studying in Berlin. My family respected me, or rather the *Neue Freie Presse* in whose golden aura I stood, too much not to grant my wish.

Of course I had no intention of 'studying' in Berlin. I called in at the university there, just as I had in Vienna, only twice in the course of a semester—once to register for lectures, the second time for certification of my alleged attendance at them. I was not looking for colleges or professors in Berlin, I wanted a greater and even more complete form of freedom. In Vienna, I still felt tied to my environment. The literary colleagues with whom I mingled almost all came from the same middle-class Jewish background as I did; in a small city where everyone knew everyone else, I was inevitably the son of a 'good' family, and I was tired of what was considered 'good' society'; I even liked the idea of decidedly bad society, an unconstrained way of life with no one checking up on me. I hadn't even looked in the university register to see who lectured on philosophy in Berlin. It was enough for me to know that modern literature was cultivated more actively and eagerly there than at home, that Dehmel and other writers of the younger generation could be met in Berlin, that new journals, cabarets and theatres were being opened, and in short, that the whole place was in a buzz.

In fact I arrived in Berlin at a very interesting moment in its history. Since 1870, when it had ceased to be the modest and by no means rich little capital of the Kingdom of Prussia and became the residence of the German Kaiser, this unassuming city on the river Spree had seen its fortunes soar to great heights. However, Berlin had not yet assumed leadership in culture and the arts. Munich, with its painters and writers, was still considered the real artistic centre; the Dresden Opera dominated music; the smaller capital cities of former princely states attracted notable artistic figures, but Vienna above all, with its centuries of tradition, concentrated cultural force, and wealth of natural talent had still, until this point, been considered greatly superior. In the last few years, however, with the rapid economic rise of Germany, all that had begun to change. Great industrial companies and prosperous families moved to Berlin, and new wealth accompanied by daring audacity opened up greater opportunities in architecture and the theatre there than in any other large German city. Under the patronage of Kaiser Wilhelm museums began to expand, the theatre found an excellent director in Otto Brahm, and the very fact that there was no real cultural tradition going back for centuries encouraged young artists to try something new. For tradition also and always means inhibition. Vienna, bound to the old ways and idolising its own past, was cautious when faced with young people and bold experiments, waiting to see what came of them. In Berlin, on the other hand, a city seeking to mould itself quickly and in its own individual form, innovation was much in demand. It was only natural, then, for young people to come thronging to Berlin from all over the Reich and even from Austria, and the talented among them were proved right by the success they achieved. Max Reinhardt of Vienna, for instance, would have had to wait patiently for a couple of decades in his native city to reach the position that he was holding in Berlin within two years.

It was at exactly this point of its change from a mere capital city to an international metropolis that I arrived in Berlin. After the rich beauty of Vienna, a legacy of our great forebears, my first impression was rather disappointing; the crucial move towards the Westend district, where a new style of architecture was to replace that of the rather ostentatious buildings of the Tiergarten, had only just begun, and architecturally uninteresting Friedrichstrasse and Leipziger Strasse, with their ponderous splendours, still formed the centre of the city. Suburbs such as Wilmersdorf, Nikolassee and Steglitz could be reached only with some difficulty by tram, and in those days visiting the austerely beautiful lakes of the March of Brandenburg still meant quite an elaborate expedition. Apart from the old Unter den Linden, there was no real centre, no place for showy parades such as the Graben in Vienna, and old Prussian habits of thrift died hard—there was no sign of elegance in general. Women went to the theatre in unfashionable home-made dresses, and wherever you went you never found the light, skilful, prodigal touch that in Vienna and Paris could make something that cost very little look enchantingly extravagant. Every detail showed the miserly economy of the period of Frederick the Great; the coffee was weak and bad because every bean was grudged, food was carelessly prepared and had no zest in it. Cleanliness and a strict, painstaking sense of order ruled here, not the musical verve of Vienna. Nothing seemed to me more typical than the contrast between my Viennese and my

Berlin landladies. The woman from whom I rented rooms in Vienna was cheerful and talkative; she did not keep everything sparkling clean, and would carelessly forget things, but she was ready and willing to oblige her tenants. My landlady in Berlin was correct and kept the place immaculate, but on receiving her first monthly bill I found every small service she had done me charged in her neat, upright hand—three pfennigs for sewing on a trouser button, twenty pfennigs for removing a splash of ink from the table top, until finally, under a strong line ruled above, the total sum I owed for such labours, they amounted to sixty-seven pfennigs in all. At first this made me smile, but more telling was the fact that after a few days I myself was infected with this Prussian passion for meticulous order, and for the first and last time in my life found myself keeping precise accounts of my expenditure.

My friends in Vienna had given me a whole series of letters of introduction, but I did not use any of them. After all, the real point of my venture was to escape the secure, bourgeois atmosphere of home and instead live free of all ties, cast entirely on my own resources. The only people I wanted to meet were those to whom I found the way through my own literary endeavours—and I wanted them to be as interesting as possible. After all, not for nothing had I read Henri Murger's *Scènes de la vie de Bohème,*[2] and at the age of twenty I was bound to want to try the bohemian life for myself.

I did not have to search long for a lively and motley assortment of friends. Back in Vienna I had been contributing for some time to the leading journal of the Berlin modernists, which went by the almost ironic title of *Das Gesellschaft*—Society—and was edited by Ludwig Jacobowski. Shortly before his early death, this young writer had founded a society called 'Die Kommenden'—The Coming Generation—a name calculated to entice the young, which met once a week on the first floor of a coffee house on Nollendorfplatz. A truly heterogeneous company met in this society, which was created on the model of the Parisian 'Closerie des Lilas'—writers and architects, snobs and journalists, young women who liked to be regarded as artists or sculptors, Russian students and ash-blonde Scandinavian girls who had come to Berlin to perfect their German. From Germany itself came representatives of all its provinces—strong-boned Westphalians, unsophisticated Bavarians, Silesian Jews, all mingling freely in fervent discussion. Now and then poems or dramas were read aloud, but for all of us our main business was getting to know each other. Amidst these young people who deliberately called themselves bohemians sat one old, grey-bearded man, a figure like Father Christmas—Peter Hille, whom we all loved and respected because he was a real writer and a real bohemian. Hille, then aged seventy, gazed kindly and guilelessly at the curious crowd of children that we were to him. He always wore his grey raincoat, which hid a frayed suit and dirty linen, and would bring badly crumpled manuscripts out of one of his pockets and read his poems aloud. They were poems like no others, more like the improvisations of a poetic genius, but too loosely formed, with too much left to chance. He wrote them in pencil, on trams or in cafés, then forgot them, and had difficulty deciphering the words on the smudged, stained piece of paper when he read them aloud. He never had any money, but he didn't care about money, sleeping the night now at one friend's, now at another's, and there was something touchingly genuine about his total unworldliness and absolute lack of ambition. It was hard to work out when and how this kindly child of nature had made his way to the big city of Berlin, and what he wanted here. However, as in fact he wanted nothing, not even to be famous or celebrated, thanks to his poetically dreamy nature he was more carefree and at ease with himself than anyone else I have ever met. Ambitious disputants shouted each other down in vociferous argument all around him; he listened quietly, did not argue with anyone, sometimes raised his glass to someone in friendly greeting, but he never joined in the conversation. You felt as if, even in the wildest tumult, words and verses were in search of each other in his shaggy and rather weary head, without ever quite touching and finding one another.

The aura of childlike truthfulness emanating from this naive poet, who is almost forgotten today even in Germany, may perhaps have distracted my attention from the chosen chairman of the Coming Generation, yet this was a man whose ideas and remarks were to have a crucial influence on the lives of countless people. Rudolf Steiner, the founder of anthroposophy, in whose honour his adherents built the most magnificent schools and academies to put his ideas into practice, was the first man I met after Theodor Herzl who was destined to show millions of human beings the way to go. In person he did not suggest a leader as strongly as Herzl, but his manner was more persuasive. There was hypnotic force in his dark eyes, and I could listen to him better and more critically if I did not look at him, for his ascetically lean face, marked by intellectual passion, was inclined to influence people by itself, men as well as women. At this time Rudolf Steiner had not yet worked out his own doctrines, but was still seeking and learning. He sometimes spoke to us about Goethe's theory of colour, and in Steiner's account of him the poet became more Faustian and Paracelsian. It was exciting to listen to him, for his learning was vast, and in particular it was magnificently wide and diverse by comparison with ours, which was confined to literature. After his lectures and many enjoyable private conversations I always went home both full of enthusiasm and slightly depressed. All the same—when I wonder now whether, at the time, I could have foretold that this young man would have such strong philosophical and ethical influence on so many people, I have to confess, to my shame, that I would not. I expected his questing spirit to do great things in science, and it would not have surprised me at all to hear of some great biological discovery made by his intuitive mind, but when many years later I saw the great Goetheanum in Dornach, the 'school of wisdom' that his followers founded for him as the Platonic academy of anthroposophy, I was rather disappointed that his influence had declined so far into the ordinary and sometimes even banal. I will not presume to pronounce judgement on anthroposophy itself, for to this day it is not perfectly clear to me what it aims for and what it means; I am inclined to think that in essence its seductive force came not from an idea but from the fascinating person of Rudolf Steiner himself. But in any case, to meet a man of such magnetic power at that early stage, when he was still imparting his ideas to younger men in a friendly manner and without dogmatism, was an inestimable benefit to me. His astonishing and at the same time profound knowledge showed me that true universality, which with schoolboy arrogance the rest of us thought we had already mastered, cannot be achieved by superficial reading and discussion, but calls for many years of ardent effort.

However, at that receptive time of life when friendships are easily made, and social and political differences have not yet become entrenched, a young man really learns better from his contemporaries in the same line of business than from his superiors. Once again I felt—although now on a higher and more international level than at school—how fruitful collective enthusiasm is. While my Viennese friends almost all came from the bourgeoisie, and indeed nine-tenths of them from the Jewish bourgeoisie, so that we were merely duplicating and multiplying our own inclinations, the young people of this new world came from very different social classes both upper and lower. One might be a Prussian aristocrat, another the son of a Hamburg shipowner, a third from a Westphalian farming family. Suddenly I was living in a circle where there was also real poverty, people in ragged clothes and worn-out shoes; I had never been near anything like it in Vienna. I sat at the same table as heavy drinkers, homosexuals and morphine addicts, I shook hands—proudly—with a well-known con man who had served a jail sentence (and later published his memoirs, thus joining our company as a writer). What I had hardly credited in realist novels was present here, teeming with life, in the little bars and cafés that I frequented, and the worse someone's reputation was the more I wanted to know him personally. This particular liking for or curiosity about people living on the edge of danger has, incidentally, stayed with me all my life; even at times when more discrimination would have been seemly, my friends used to point out that I seemed to like mingling with amoral and unreliable people whose company might be compromising. Perhaps the very fact that I came from a solidly established background, and felt to some extent that this 'security' complex weighed me down, made me more likely to be fascinated by those who almost recklessly squandered their lives, their time, their money, their health and reputation—passionate monomaniacs obsessed by aimless existence for its own sake—and perhaps readers may notice this preference of mine for intense, intemperate characters in my novels and novellas. And then there was the charm of the exotic and outlandish; almost everyone presented my questing mind with a gift from a strange new world. For the first time I met a genuine Eastern Jew, the graphic artist E M Lilien, son of a poor Orthodox master turner from Drohobycz, and so I encountered an aspect of Jewishness previously unknown to me in its force and tough fanaticism. A young Russian translated for my benefit the finest passages from the *Brothers Karamazov*, unknown in Germany at the time; a young Swedish woman first introduced me to the pictures of Munch; I visited painters' studios to observe their technique (admittedly they were not very good painters), a believer in spiritualism took me to seances—I sensed the diversity of a thousand forms of life, and never tired of it. The intense interest which at school I had shown only in literary form, in rhymes, verses and words, was now bent on human beings. From morning to night, I was always with new and different acquaintances in Berlin, fascinated, disappointed, even sometimes cheated by them. I think that in ten years elsewhere I never have enjoyed such a variety of intellectual company as I did in that one short semester in Berlin, the first of my total freedom.

It would seem only logical for my creative impulse to have been enhanced to a high degree by all this stimulation. In fact exactly the opposite happened—much of my self-confidence, greatly boosted at first by the intellectual exhilaration of my schooldays, was now draining away. Four months after the appearance of that immature volume of poetry I couldn't understand how I had ever summoned up the courage to publish it. I still thought the verses good in themselves, skilful, some of them even remarkably craftsmanlike, the end result of my ambitious enjoyment of playing about with form, but there was a false ring to their sentimentality. In the same way, after this encounter with reality I felt there was a whiff of scented notepaper about my first novellas. Written in total ignorance of real life, they employed other people's techniques at second hand. A novel that I had brought to Berlin with me, finished except for the last chapter, was soon heating my stove, for my faith in my powers and those of my class at school in Vienna had suffered a severe setback after this first look at real life. I felt as if I were still a schoolboy and had been told to move two classes lower down. After that first volume of poems there was a gap of six years before I published a second, and only after three or four years did I publish my first prose work. Following the advice of Dehmel, to whom I am still grateful, I used my time translating from foreign languages, which I still regard as the best way for a young writer to gain a deeper, more creative understanding of the spirit of his own mother tongue. I translated Baudelaire, some poems by Verlaine, Keats, William Morris, a short play by Charles Van Lerberghe, and a novel by Camille Lemonnier[3] to get my hand in. The more personal turns of phrase in every foreign language initially present a translator with difficulties, and that in itself is a challenge to a young writer's powers of expression which will not come into play unsought, and this struggle to persist in wresting its essence from the foreign language and making your own equally expressive has always given me a special kind of artistic pleasure. Since this quiet and rather unappreciated work calls for patience and stamina, virtues that I had tended to ignore out of a sense of daring ease while I was at school, it became particularly dear to me, because in this modest activity of interpreting illustrious works of art I felt certain, for the first time, that I was doing something really meaningful which justified my existence.

I was now clear in my mind about the path I would tread for the next few years; I would see and learn a great deal, and only then would I really begin. I did not plan to present myself to the world with rashly premature publications—first I wanted to know what the world was all about! The astringency of Berlin had only increased my thirst for such knowledge. And

I wondered what country to visit that summer. I opted for Belgium, which had seen a great artistic upturn around the turn of the century, in some ways even outshining France.

Khnopff and Rops in painting, Constantin Meunier and Minne in sculpture, van der Velde in arts and crafts, Maeterlinck, Eekhoud and Lemonnier in literature set high standards for modern Europe. But above all I was fascinated by Emile Verhaeren, because he showed an entirely new way ahead in poetry. He was still unknown in Germany—where for a long time the established critics confused him with Verlaine, just as they got Rolland mixed up with Rostand—and it could be said that I discovered him for myself. And to come to love someone in that way always redoubles one's affection.

Perhaps I should add a little parenthesis here. Today we get too much experience, and get it too fast, to remember it well, and I do not know if the name of Emile Verhaeren still means anything. Verhaeren was the first Francophone poet to try doing for Europe what Walt Whitman did for America—declare his belief in the present and the future. He had begun to love the modern world and wanted to conquer it for literature. While other writers regarded machines as evil, cities as ugly, the present as unpoetic, he felt enthusiasm for every new discovery and technical achievement, and his own enthusiasm spurred him on; he took a close interest in science so that he could feel that passion more strongly. The minor poems of his early work led on to great, flowing hymns. "*Admirez-vous les uns les autres*", marvel at one another, was his message to the nations of Europe. All the optimism of our generation, incomprehensible today at the time of our terrible relapse, found its first poetic expression in him, and some of his best poems will long bear witness to the Europe of the time and the kind of humanity that we dreamt of then.

I had really gone to Brussels on purpose to meet Verhaeren, but Camille Lemonnier, the fine and now unjustly forgotten author of *Un Mâle*, one of whose novels I had myself translated into German, told me regretfully that Verhaeren seldom left the little village where he lived to come to Brussels, and was not in that city now. To make up for my disappointment, he gave me valuable introductions to other Belgian artists. So I saw the old master Constantin Meunier, the greatest sculptor of the time to depict labour and a heroic labourer in his own field, and after him van der Stappen,[4] whose name is now almost forgotten in the history of art. But what a friendly man that small, chubby-cheeked Fleming was, and how warmly he and his tall, broad, cheerful Dutch wife welcomed their young visitor. He showed me his work, and we talked about art and literature for a long time that bright morning. The couple's kindness soon banished any awkwardness on my part. I told them frankly how disappointed I had been in Brussels to miss seeing the very man for whose sake I had really come to Belgium, Emile Verhaeren.

Had I said too much? Had I said something silly? I noticed both van der Stappen and his wife smiling slightly and glancing surreptitiously at each other. I felt that my words had set off some secret understanding between them. Feeling embarrassed, I said I must be going, but they wouldn't hear of it, and insisted on my staying to lunch. Once again that odd smile passed between their eyes. I felt that if there was some kind of secret here, then it was a friendly one, and was happy to abandon my original plan of going on to Waterloo.

It was soon lunchtime, we were already in the dining room— on the ground floor, as in all Belgian houses—where you looked out on the street through stained-glass panes, when suddenly a shadowy figure stopped, sharply outlined, on the other side of the window. Knuckles tapped on the stained glass, and the doorbell rang a loud peal. "*Le voilà*," said Mme van der Stappen, getting to her feet, and in he came with a strong, heavy tread. It was Verhaeren himself. I recognised the face that had long been familiar to me from his pictures at first glance. Verhaeren was their guest to lunch today, as he very often was, and when they heard that I had been looking for him in vain they had agreed, in that quick exchange of glances, not to tell me but to let his arrival take me by surprise. And now there he was before me, smiling at the success of their trick when he heard about it. For the first time I felt the firm grip of his sinewy hand, for the first time I saw his clear and kindly gaze. He came—as always—into the house as if full of vigour and enthusiasm. Even as he ate heartily, he kept talking. He had been to see friends, he told us, they had gone to a gallery, he still felt inspired by that visit. This was his usual manner of arrival, his state of mind intensified by chance experiences anywhere and everywhere, and this enthusiasm was his established habit. Like a flame, it leapt again and again from his lips, and he was master of the art of emphasising his words with graphic gestures. With the first thing he said, he reached into you because he was perfectly open, accessible to every newcomer, rejecting nothing, ready for everyone. He sent his whole being, you might say, out to meet you again and again, and I saw him make that overwhelming, stormy impression on many other people after experiencing it for myself on that first meeting. He knew nothing about me, but he already trusted me just because he had heard that I appreciated his works.

After lunch and that first delightful surprise came a second. Van der Stappen, who had long been meaning to fulfil an old wish of his own and Verhaeren's, had been working for days on a bust of the poet, and today was to be the last sitting. My presence, said van der Stappen, was a very lucky chance, because he positively needed someone to talk to Verhaeren—who was only too inclined to fidget—while he sat for the sculptor so that his face would be animated as he talked and listened. And so I looked deeply into his face for two hours, that unforgettable face with its high forehead, ploughed deeply by the wrinkled furrows of his bad years, his brown, rust-coloured hair falling over it, the hard, stern structure of his features surrounded by brownish weather-beaten skin, his chin jutting like a rock and above the narrow lips, large and lavish, his drooping moustache in the Vercingetorix style. All his nervousness was in his hands—those lean, firm, fine and yet strong hands where the veins throbbed strongly under the thin skin. The whole weight of his will was expressed in his broad, rustic shoulders; the intelligent, bony head almost seemed too small for them. Only when he was moving did you see his strength. If I look at the bust of him now—and van der Stappen never did anything better than the work of that day—I know how true to life it is, and how fully it catches the essence of the man. It is documentary evidence of literary stature, a monument to unchanging power.

In those three hours I learnt to love the man as I have loved him all the rest of my life. There was a confidence in him that did not for a moment seem self-satisfied. He did not mind about money; he would rather live in the country than write a line meant only for the day and the hour. He did not mind about success either, did not try to increase it by granting concessions or doing favours or showing cameraderie—his friends of the same cast of mind were enough for him. He was even independent of the temptation so dangerous to a famous man when fame at last came to him at the zenith of his life. He remained open in every sense, hampered by no inhibitions, confused by no vanity, a free and happy man, easily giving vent to every enthusiasm. When you were with him, you felt inspired in your own will to live.

So there he was in the flesh before me, young as I then was—a poet such as I had hoped to find him, exactly as I had dreamt of him. And even in that first hour of our personal acquaintance my decision was taken; I would put myself at the service of this man and his work. It was a bold decision, for this hymnodist of Europe was little known at the time in Europe itself, and I knew in advance that translating his monumental body of poetry and his three-verse dramas would keep me from writing my own work for two or three years. But as I determined to devote all my power, time and passion to someone else's work, I was giving myself the best thing imaginable—a moral mission. My vague seeking, my own attempts, now had a point. And if I am asked today to advise a young writer who has not yet made up his mind what way to go, I would try to persuade him to devote himself first to the work of someone greater, interpreting or translating him. If you are a beginner there is more security in such self-sacrifice than in your own creativity, and nothing that you ever do with all your heart is done in vain.

In the two years that I spent almost exclusively in translating the poetry of Verhaeren and preparing to write a biography of him, I travelled a good deal at various times, sometimes to give public lectures. And I had already received unexpected thanks for my apparently thankless devotion to Verhaeren's work; his friends abroad noticed me, and soon became my friends too. One day, for instance, the delightful Swede Ellen Key came to see me—a woman who, with extraordinary courage in those still blind and backward times, was fighting for the emancipation of women, and in her book *The Century of the Child* pointed a warning finger, long before Freud, at the mental vulnerability of young people. Through her, I was introduced to the poetic circle in Italy of Giovanni Cena, and made an important friend in the Norwegian Johan Bojer. Georg Brandes, international master of the history of literature, took an interest in me, and thanks to my promotion of it the name of Verhaeren began to be better known in Germany than in his native land. Kainz, that great actor, and Moissi gave public recitations of his poems in my translation. Max Reinhardt produced Verhaeren's *Les*

Moines—The Monks—on the German stage. I had good reason to feel pleased.

But now it was time to think of myself and remember that I had taken on other duties as well as those to Verhaeren. I had to bring my university career to a successful conclusion and take my doctorate in philosophy home. Now it was a matter of catching up within a few months with the entire scholastic material on which more conscientious students had been labouring for almost four years. With Erwin Guido Kolbenheyer, a literary friend of my youth who may not be too happily remembered today because he was one of the acknowledged public writers and academics of Hitler's Germany, I crammed by night. But the examination was not made difficult for me. In a private preliminary conversation the kindly professor, who knew too much about me from my public literary activities to trouble me with details, said with a smile, "I expect you'd rather not be tested in the field of exact logic," and then gently led me into spheres where he knew I was sure of myself. It was the first time that I had to take an examination, and I hope the last, and I passed with distinction. Now I was outwardly free, and all the years from then until the present day have been given to my struggle to remain equally free in my mind—a struggle that, in our times, is becoming ever harder.

NOTES

1   Detlev von Liliencron, pseudonym of Friedrich, Baron von
    Liliencron, poet, 1844-1909. Richard Dehmel, 1863-1920, poet. A
    close friend of Liliencron, and much influenced by Nietzsche. Otto
    Julius Bierbaum, 1865-1910, poet, novelist and dramatist. Alfred
    Mombert, 1872-1942, poet.

2   *Scenes from Bohemian Life*, the novel on which Puccini's opera *La Bohème*
    is based.

3   Charles Van Lerberghe, 1861-1907, Belgian Symbolist poet. Camille
    Lemonnier, 1844-1913, Belgian poet and novelist.

4   Charles Van der Stappen, 1843-1910, Belgian sculptor.

BRIGHTNESS AND SHADOWS
OVER EUROPE

I HAD NOW LIVED THROUGH ten years of the new century; I had seen India, part of America, and I began thinking of Europe with a new and better-informed sense of pleasure. I never loved our old world *more* than in those last years before the First World War; I never hoped more for a united Europe; I never believed more in its future than at that time, when we thought there was a new dawn in sight. But its red hue was really the firelight of the approaching international conflagration.

Today's generation has grown up amidst disasters, crises, and the failure of systems. The young see war as a constant possibility to be expected almost daily, and it may be difficult to describe to them the optimism and confidence in the world that we felt when we ourselves were young at the turn of the century. Forty years of peace had strengthened national economies, technology had speeded up the pace of life, scientific discoveries had been a source of pride to the spirit of our own generation. The upswing now beginning could be felt to almost the same extent in all European countries. Cities were more attractive and densely populated year by year; the Berlin of 1905 was not like the city I had known in 1901. From being the capital of a princely state it had become an international metropolis, which in turn paled beside the Berlin of 1910. Vienna, Milan, Paris, London, Amsterdam—whenever you came back to them you were surprised and delighted. The streets were broader and finer, the public buildings more imposing, the shops more elegant. Everything conveyed a sense of the growth and wider distribution of wealth. Even we writers noticed it from the editions of our books printed; in the space of ten years the number of copies printed per edition tripled, then multiplied by fivefold and by tenfold. There were new theatres, libraries and museums everywhere. Domestic facilities such as bathrooms and telephones that used to be the prerogative of a few select circles became available to the lower middle class, and now that hours of work were shorter than before, the proletariat had its own share in at least the minor pleasures and comforts of life. There was progress everywhere. Who dared, won. If you bought a house, a rare book, a picture you saw its value rise; the bolder and more ambitious the ideas behind an enterprise, the more certain it was to succeed. There was a wonderfully carefree atmosphere abroad in the world—for what was going to interrupt this growth, what could stand in the way of the vigour constantly drawing new strength from its own momentum? Europe had never been stronger, richer or more beautiful, had never believed more fervently in an even better future, and no one except a few shrivelled old folk still bewailed the passing of the 'good old days'.

And not only were the cities more beautiful, their inhabitants too were more attractive and healthier, thanks to sporting activities, better nutrition, shorter working hours and a closer link with nature. People had discovered that up in the mountains winter, once a dismal season to be spent gloomily playing cards in taverns or feeling bored as you sat around in overheated rooms, was a source of filtered sunlight, nectar for the lungs that sent blood coursing deliciously just beneath the skin. The mountains, the lakes and the sea no longer seemed so far away. Bicycles, motor cars, electric railways had shrunk distance and given the world a new sense of space. On Sundays thousands and tens of thousands, clad in brightly coloured sportswear, raced down the snowy slopes on skis and toboggans; sports centres and swimming baths were built everywhere. You could see the change clearly in those swimming baths—while in my own youth a really fine figure of a man stood out among all the bull-necked, paunchy or pigeon-chested specimens, nowadays athletically agile young men, tanned by the sun and fit from all their sporting activities, competed cheerfully with each other as they did in classical antiquity. Only the most poverty-stricken stayed at home now on a Sunday; all the young people went walking, climbing or competing in all kinds of sports. When they went on holiday they did not, as in my parents' time, find somewhere to stay near the city, or at the most no further away than the Salzkammergut. Their curiosity about the world had been aroused; they wanted to see if it was as beautiful everywhere, or maybe beautiful in a different way in other places, and while once only the privileged few travelled abroad, now bank clerks and small tradesmen went away to Italy or France. Foreign travel had become cheaper and more comfortable, but above all a new bold, adventurous attitude made travellers willing to venture further afield, less thrifty, less anxious—indeed, anxiety was something to be ashamed of. That whole generation was determined to be more youthful; unlike young people in the world of my parents, everyone was proud of youth. Suddenly beards disappeared, first in the younger men, then shaved off by their elders, imitating them so as not to be thought of as old. Youthful freshness was more desirable than dignity. Women threw away the corsets that had constricted their breasts, stopped fearing fresh air and sunlight and gave up sunshades and veils; they shortened their skirts so that they could move more freely when they played tennis, and they were not shy about showing a well-turned pair of legs. Fashions became more and more natural, men wore breeches, women dared to ride astride, and the sexes stopped concealing themselves from each other. There was more freedom as well as more beauty in the world.

It was the health and self-confidence of the generation after ours that also laid claim to freedom for itself in manners and morals. For the first time, you saw young girls enjoying excursions and sporting activities in open and confident friendship with young men, and without a governess going along as chaperone. They were no longer timid and prudish; they knew what they wanted and what they did not. Escaping the anxious authority of their parents, earning their own living as secretaries or clerks, they took control of their own lives. This new, healthier freedom led to a clear decrease in prostitution, the sole permitted erotic institution of the old world, and prudery of every kind now seemed old-fashioned. Increasingly, the wooden partitions in swimming baths that used to divide the gentlemen's and ladies' pools from each other were taken down. Women and men were not ashamed to show their figures any more. In those ten years there was more freedom, informality and lack of inhibition than there had been in the entire preceding century.

For the world was moving to a different rhythm. A year—so much could happen in a year now! Inventions and discoveries followed hard on each other's heels, and each in turn swiftly became a general good. For the first time the nations all felt in common what was for the benefit of all. On the day when the Zeppelin[1] rose in the air for its first flight, I was on my way to Belgium and happened to be in Strasburg where, to shouts of jubilation from the crowd, it circled the Münster as if bowing to the thousand-year-old cathedral while it hovered in the air. That evening, at the Verhaerens', news came that the airship had crashed in Echterdingen. Verhaeren had tears in his eyes, and was badly upset. Belgian though he was, this German catastrophe did not leave him unmoved; it was as a European, a man of our time, that he felt for our common victory over the elements as well as this common setback. When Blériot made the first cross-Channel flight in an aeroplane, we rejoiced in Vienna as if he were a hero of our own nation; pride in the triumphs of our technology and science, which succeeded one another by the hour, had led for the first time to a European sense of community, the development of a European identity. How pointless, we said to ourselves, frontiers were if it was child's play for any aircraft to cross them, how provincial and artificial were customs barriers and border guards, how contrary to the spirit of our times that clearly wished for closer links and international fraternity!

This upward surge of feeling was no less remarkable than the upward rise of aircraft; I feel sorry for all who did not live through these last years of European confidence while they were still young themselves. For the air around us is not a dead and empty void, it has in it the rhythm and vibration of the time. We absorb them unconsciously into our bloodstream as the air carries them deep into our hearts and minds. Perhaps, ungrateful as human beings are, we did not realise at the time how strongly and securely the wave bore us up. But only those who knew that time of confidence in the world know that everything since has been regression and gloom.

That world was a wonderful tonic, its strength reaching our hearts from all the coasts of Europe. At the same time, however, although we did not guess it, what delighted us was dangerous. The stormy wind of pride and confidence sweeping over Europe brought clouds with it. Perhaps the upward move-ment had come too fast, states and cities had made themselves powerful too swiftly—and an awareness of having power always leads states, like men, to use or misuse it. France was extremely wealthy, yet it wanted still more, it wanted another colony although it did not have enough people for the old ones, and it almost went to war over Morocco. Italy had its eye on Cyrenaica;[2] Austria annexed Bosnia; Serbia and Bulgaria advanced on Turkey; and Germany, although inactive for the moment, was flexing its claws to strike in anger. All the states were suffering a rush of blood to the head. Everywhere, and at the same time, the productive wish for consolidation at home began to develop, like an infectious illness, into a greedy desire for expansion. High-earning French industrialists agitated against their German counterparts, who were also rolling in riches, because both Krupp and Schneider-Creusot wanted to be able to supply more artillery. The Hamburg shipping industry, which earned huge dividends, was vying with shipping based in Southampton, Hungarian and Bulgarian agriculture were in competition, one group of companies was set against all the rest—the economic situation had maddened them all in their frantic wish to get their hands on more and more. If today, thinking it over calmly, we wonder why Europe went to war in 1914, there is not one sensible reason to be found, nor even any real occasion for the war. There were no ideas involved, it was not really about drawing minor borderlines; I can explain it only, thinking of that excess of power, by seeing it as a tragic consequence of the internal dynamism that had built up during those forty years of peace, and now demanded release. Every state suddenly felt that it was strong, and forgot that other states felt exactly the same; all states wanted even more, and wanted some of what the others already had. The worst of it was that the very thing we loved most, our common optimism, betrayed us, for everyone thought that everyone else would back down at the last minute, and so the diplomats began their game of mutual bluff. In four or five instances, for instance in Agadir and in the Balkan Wars, it was still only a game, but the great coalitions drew closer and closer together and became increasingly militant. Germany introduced a war tax in the middle of peacetime, France extended its term of military service. Finally the accumulated head of steam had to be released. And the weather over the Balkans showed the way the wind was blowing as the clouds approached Europe.

There was no panic yet, but there was a constant sense of smouldering uneasiness; we still felt only slightly uncomfortable when shots rang out from the Balkans. Was war really going to descend on us, when we had no idea why? Slowly—but too slowly, too hesitantly, as we now know—the forces rejecting war came together. There was the Socialist Party, millions of people on all sides, with a programme opposing war; there were powerful Catholic groups under the leadership of the Pope and several international groups of companies; there were a few reasonable politicians who spoke out against any undercover dealings. We writers also ranged ourselves against war, although as usual we spoke in isolation, expressing ourselves as individuals rather than closing ranks to speak firmly as an organisation. Most intellectuals, unfortunately, adopted an indifferent and passive stance, for our optimism meant that the problem of war, with all its moral consequences, had not yet entered our personal field of vision—you will not find a single discussion of the principles involved, or a single passionate warning, in the major works of the prominent writers of that time. We thought we were doing enough if we thought in European terms and forged fraternal links internationally, stating in our own sphere—which had only indirect influence on current events—that we were in favour of the ideal of peaceful understanding and intellectual brotherhood crossing linguistic and national borders. And the younger generation was more strongly attached than anyone to this European ideal. In Paris, I found my friend Bazalgette surrounded by a group of young people who, in contrast to the older generation, had abjured all kinds of narrow-minded nationalism and imperialist aggression. Jules Romains, who was to write a great work on Europe at war, Georges Duhamel, Charles Vildrac, Durtain, René Arcos,[3] Jean-Richard Bloch, meeting first in the Abbaye and then in the Effort Libre groups, were passionate in their pioneering work for the future unity of Europe, and when put to the crucial test of war, were implacable in their abhorrence of every kind of militarism. These were young people of such courage, talent and moral determination as France has not often produced. In Germany, it was Franz Werfel with his collection of poems entitled *Der Weltfreund*—Friend of the World—who promoted international fraternity most strongly. René Schickele, an Alsatian whose fate it therefore was to stand between the two opposing nations, worked passionately for understanding; G A Borgese sent us comradely greetings from Italy, and encouragement came from the Scandinavian and Slavonic countries. "Come and visit us!" one great Russian author wrote to me. "Show the pan-Slavists who urge us to go to war that you are against it in Austria!" How we all loved our time, a time that carried us forward on its wings; how we all loved Europe! But that overconfident faith in the future which, we were sure, would avert madness at the last minute, was also our own fault. We had certainly failed to look at the writing on the wall with enough distrust, but should not right-minded young people be trusting rather than suspicious? We trusted Jaurès and the Socialist International, we thought railway workers would blow up the tracks rather than let their comrades be loaded into trains to be sent to the front as cannon fodder; we relied on women to refuse to see their children and husbands sacrificed to the idol Moloch; we were convinced that the intellectual and moral power of Europe would assert itself triumphantly at the critical last moment. Our common idealism, the optimism that had come from progress, meant that we failed to see and speak out strongly enough against our common danger.

Moreover, what we lacked was an organiser who could bring the forces latent in us together effectively. We had only one prophet among us, a single man who looked ahead and saw what was to come, and the curious thing about it was that he lived among us, and it was a long time before we knew anything about him, although he had been sent by Fate as a leader. To me, finding him in the nick of time was a crucial stroke of luck, and it was hard to find him too, since he lived in the middle of Paris far from the hurly-burly of *la foire sur la place*.[4] Anyone who sets out to write an honest history of French literature in the twentieth century will be unable to ignore a remarkable phenomenon—the names of all kinds of writers were lauded to the skies in the Parisian newspapers of the time, except for the three most important of them, who were either disregarded or mentioned in the wrong context. From 1900 to 1914 I never saw the name of Paul Valéry mentioned as a poet in *Le Figaro* or *Le Matin*; Marcel Proust was considered a mere dandy who frequented the Paris salons, and Romain Rolland was thought of as a knowledgeable musicologist. They were almost fifty before the first faint light of fame touched their names, and their great work was hidden in darkness in the most enquiring city in the world.

*

It was pure chance that I discovered Romain Rolland at the right time. A Russian woman sculptor living in Florence had invited me to tea, to show me her work and try her hand at a sketch of me. I arrived punctually at four, forgetting that she was, after all, a Russian, so time and punctuality meant nothing to her. An old babushka who, I discovered, had been her mother's nurse, took me into the studio—the most picturesque thing about it was its disorder—and asked me to wait. In all there were four small sculptures standing around, and I had seen them all within two minutes. So as not to waste time, I picked up a book, or rather a couple of brown-covered journals lying about the studio. These were entitled *Cahiers de la Quinzaine*,[5] and I remembered having heard that title in Paris before. But who could keep track of the many little magazines that sprang up all over the country, short-lived idealistic flowers, and then disappeared again? I leafed through one of them, containing *L'Aube*, by Romain Rolland, and began to read, feeling more astonished and interested as I went on. Who was this Frenchman who knew Germany so well? Soon I was feeling grateful to my Russian friend for her unpunctuality. When she finally arrived, my first question was, "Who is this Romain Rolland?" She couldn't give me any very clear information, and only when I had acquired other issues of the magazine (the next was still in production) did I know that here at last was a work serving not just one European nation, but all of them and the fraternal connection between them. Here was the man, here was the writer who brought all the moral forces into play—affectionate understanding and an honest desire to find out more. He showed a sense of justice based on experience, and an inspiring faith in the unifying power of art. While the rest of us were squandering our efforts on small declarations of faith, he had set to work quietly and patiently to show the nations to one another through their most appealing individual qualities. This was the first consciously European novel being written at the time, the first vital call for fraternity, and it would be more effective in reaching a wider readership than Verhaeren's hymns, and in being more cogent than all the pamphlets and protests. What we had all unconsciously been hoping and longing for was being quietly written here.

The first thing I did in Paris was to ask about him, bearing in mind what Goethe had said: "He has learnt, he can teach us." I asked my friends about him. Verhaeren thought he remembered a play called *The Wolves* that had been staged at the socialist Théâtre du Peuple. Bazalgette had heard that Rolland was a musicologist and had written a short book on Beethoven. In the catalogue of the Bibliothèque Nationale I found a dozen works of his about old and modern music, and seven or eight plays, all of which had appeared under the imprint of small publishing houses or in the *Cahiers de la Quinzaine*. Finally, by way of a first approach to him, I sent him a book of my own. A letter soon arrived inviting me to visit him, and thus began a friendship that, together with my relationships with Freud and Verhaeren, was one of the most fruitful and often crucial of my life.

Notable days in our lives have a brighter aura about them than the ordinary kind. So I now remember that first visit with great clarity. I climbed five narrow, winding flights of stairs in an unpretentious building in the boulevard Montparnasse, and even outside the door I felt a special kind of stillness; the noise in the street sounded hardly any louder than the wind blowing in the trees of an old monastery garden below the windows. Rolland opened the door and took me into his small room, which was crammed with books up to the ceiling. For the first time I saw his remarkably bright blue eyes, the clearest and at the same time kindest eyes I ever saw in any human being, eyes that drew colour and fire from his inmost feelings in conversation, darkly shadowed in sorrow, appearing to grow deeper when he was thinking, sparkling with excitement—those unique eyes, under lids that were a little overtired, easily became red-rimmed when he had been reading or staying up late, but could shine radiantly in a congenial and happy light. I observed his figure with a little anxiety. Tall and thin, he stooped slightly as he walked, as if the countless hours at his desk had weighed his head down; his very pale complexion and angular features made him look rather unwell. He spoke very quietly and was sparing of physical effort in general; he almost never went out walking, he ate little, did not drink or smoke, but later I realised, with admiration, what great stamina there was in that ascetic frame, what a capacity for intellectual work lay behind his apparent debility. He would write for hours at his small desk, which was piled high with papers; he would read in bed for hours, never allowing his exhausted body more than four or five hours of sleep, and the only relaxation in which he indulged was music. He played the piano very well, with a delicate touch that I shall never forget, caressing the keys as if to entice rather than force the notes out of them. No virtuoso—and I have heard Max Reger, Busoni and Bruno Walter playing in small gatherings—gave me such a sense of direct communication with the master composers he loved.

His knowledge was very wide, putting most of us to shame; although he really lived only through his reading eyes; he had a fine command of literature, philosophy, history, and the problems of all nations at all times. He knew every bar of classical music; he was familiar with even the least-known works of Galuppi and Telemann, and with the music of sixth-rate or seventh-rate composers as well, yet he took a passionate interest in all events of the present day. The world was reflected in this monastic cell of his as if in a camera obscura. He had been on familiar terms with the great men of his time, had been a pupil of Renan, a guest in Wagner's house, a friend of Jaurès. Tolstoy had written him a famous letter that would go on record as human appreciation of his literary works. Here—and this always rejoices my heart—I sensed a human and moral superiority, an inner freedom without pride, something to be taken for granted in a strong mind. At first sight, and time has proved me right, I recognised him as the man who would be the conscience of Europe in its time of crisis. We talked about his *Jean-Christophe* novels. Rolland told me that he had tried to make the work fulfil a triple purpose—conveying his gratitude to music, his commitment to the cause of European unity, and an appeal to the nations to stop and think. Now we must all do what we could in our own positions, our own countries, our own languages. It was time, he said, to be more and more on our guard. The forces working for hatred, in line with their baser nature, were more violent and aggressive than the forces of reconciliation, and there were material interests behind them which, of their very nature, were more unscrupulous than ours. I found such grief over the fragility of earthly structures doubly moving in a man whose entire work celebrated the immortality of art. "It can bring comfort to us as individuals," he replied to me, "but it can do nothing against stark reality."

This was in 1913. It was the first conversation that showed me it was our duty not to confront the possibility of a European war passively and unprepared. When the crucial moment came, nothing gave Rolland such great moral superiority over everyone else as the way he had already, and painfully, strengthened his mind to face it in advance. Perhaps the rest of our circle had done something too. I had translated many works, I had promoted the best writers in the countries that were our neighbours, I had accompanied Verhaeren on a lecture tour all over Germany in 1912, and the tour had turned out to be a symbolic demonstration of Franco-German fraternity. In Hamburg Verhaeren and Dehmel, respectively the greatest poets of their time writing in French and German, had embraced in public. I had interested Reinhardt in Verhaeren's new play; our collaboration on both sides had never been warmer, more intense or more unconstrained, and in many hours of enthusiasm we entertained the illusion that we had shown the world the way that would save it. The world, however, took little notice of such literary manifestations, but went its own way to ruin. There was a kind of electrical crackling in the structural woodwork as if of invisible friction. Now and then a spark would fly up—the Zabern Affair,[6] the crises in Albania, the occasional unfortunate interview. Never more than a spark, but each one could have caused the accumulation of explosive material to blow up. We in Austria were keenly aware that we were at the heart of the area of unrest. In 1910 Emperor Franz Joseph passed the age of eighty. The old man, an icon in his own lifetime, could not last much longer, and a mystical belief began to spread among the public at large that after his death there would be no way to prevent the dissolution of the thousand-year-old monarchy. At home, the pressure of opposing nationalities grew; abroad Italy, Serbia, Romania and to some extent even Germany were waiting to divide up the Austrian empire. The war in the Balkans, where Krupp and Schneider-Creusot competed in trying out their artillery on 'human material', just as later the Germans and Italians tried out their aeroplanes during the Spanish Civil War, drew us further and further into the raging torrent. We kept waking with a start, but to breathe again and again, with a sigh of relief, "Not this time. Not yet, and let us hope never!"

As everyone knows, it is a thousand times easier to reconstruct the facts of what happened at a certain time than its intellectual atmosphere. That atmosphere is reflected not in official events but, most conspicuously, in small, personal episodes of the kind that I am going to recount here. To be honest, I did not believe that war was coming at the time. But I twice had what might be called a waking dream of it, and woke with my mind in great turmoil. The first time was over the 'Redl Affair', which like many of those episodes that form a backdrop to history is not widely known.

Personally I knew Colonel Redl, the central character in one of the most complex of espionage dramas, only slightly. He lived a street away from me in the same district of Vienna, and once, in the café where this comfortable-looking gentleman, who appreciated the pleasures of the senses, was smoking his cigar, I was introduced to him by my friend Public Prosecutor T. After that we greeted each other when we met. But it was only later that I discovered how much secrecy surrounds us in the midst of our daily lives, and how little we really know about those who are close to us. This colonel, who looked very much the usual capable Austrian officer, was in the confidence of the heir to the throne. It was his important responsibility to head the army's secret service and thwart the activities of their opposing counterparts. It came out that during the crisis of the war in the Balkans in 1912, when Russia and Austria were mobilising to move against each other, the most important secret item in the hands of the Austrian army, the 'marching plan', had been sold to Russia. If war had come, this would have been nothing short of disastrous, for the Russians now knew in advance, move by move, every tactical manoeuvre for attack planned by the Austrian army. The panic set off among the General Staff of the army by this act of treachery was terrible. It was up to Colonel Redl, as the man in charge, to apprehend the traitor, who must be somewhere in the very highest places. The Foreign Ministry, not entirely trusting the competence of the military authorities, also let it be known without first informing the General Staff—a typical example of the jealous rivalry of those organisations—that they were going to follow the matter up independently, and to this end gave the police the job of taking various measures, including the opening of letters from abroad sent poste restante, regardless of the principle that such correspondence was strictly private.

One day, then, a post office received a letter from the Russian border station at Podvolokzyska to a poste-restante address code-named 'Opera Ball'. On being opened, it proved to contain no letter, but six or eight new Austrian thousand-crown notes. This suspicious find was reported at once to the chief of police, who issued instructions for a detective to be stationed at the post-office counter to arrest the person who came to claim the suspect letter on the spot.

For a moment it looked as if the tragedy was about to turn into Viennese farce. A gentleman turned up at midday, asking for the letter addressed to 'Opera Ball'. The clerk at the counter instantly gave a concealed signal to alert the detective. But the detective had just gone out for a snack, and when he came back all that anyone could say for certain was that the unknown gentleman had taken a horse-drawn cab and driven off in no-one-knew-what direction. However, the second act of this Viennese comedy soon began. In the time of those fashionable, elegant cabs, each of them a carriage and pair, the driver of the cab considered himself far too good to clean his cab with his own hands. So at every cab rank there was a man whose job it was to feed the horses and wash the carriage. This man, fortunately, had noticed the number of the cab that had just driven off. In quarter-of-an-hour all police offices had been alerted and the cab had been found. Its driver described the gentleman who had taken the vehicle to the Café Kaiserhof, where I often met Colonel Redl, and moreover, by pure good luck, the pocketknife that the cabby's unknown fare had used to open the envelope was found still in the cab. Detectives hurried straight off to the Café Kaiserhof. By then the gentleman described by the cabby had left, but the waiters explained, as if it were the most natural thing in the world, that he could only be their regular customer Colonel Redl, and he had just gone back to the Hotel Klomser.

The detective in charge of the case froze. The mystery was solved. Colonel Redl, the top espionage chief in the Austrian army, was also a spy in the pay of Russia. He had not only sold Austrian secrets and the army's marching plan, it also instantly became clear why, over the last year, the Austrian agents he sent to Russia had been regularly arrested, tried and found guilty. Frantic telephone conversations began, finally reaching Franz Conrad von Hötzendorf, Chief of General Staff of the Austrian army. An eyewitness of this scene told me that on hearing the first few words he turned white as a sheet. Phone calls to the Hofburg palace ensued, discussion following discussion. What should be done next? The police had now made sure that Colonel Redl could not get away. When he was leaving the Hotel Klomser, and was giving the hotel porter some instructions, a detective unobtrusively approached him, offered him the pocketknife and asked, in civil tones, "Did you happen to leave this pocketknife in your cab, Colonel?" At that moment Redl knew that the game was up. Wherever he turned, he saw the familiar faces of secret policemen keeping watch on him, and when he returned to the hotel, two officers followed him up to his room and put a revolver down in front of him, for by now a decision had been reached in the Hofburg—the end of an affair showing the Austrian army in such an ignominious light would be best hushed up. The two officers stayed on duty outside Redl's room in the Hotel Klomser until two in the morning. Only then did they hear the sound of the revolver being fired inside the room.

Next day a brief obituary of the highly regarded officer Colonel Redl, who had died suddenly, appeared in the evening papers. But too many people had been involved in tracking him down for the secret to be kept. Gradually, moreover, details that explained a great deal in psychological terms came to light. Unknown to any of his superiors or colleagues, Colonel Redl's proclivities had been homosexual, and for years he had been a victim of blackmailers who finally drove him to this desperate means of extricating himself from their toils. A shudder of horror passed through the entire army. Everyone knew that if war came, this one man could have cost the country the lives of hundreds of thousands, bringing the monarchy to the brink of the abyss. Only then did we Austrians realise how very close we had been to world war already during the past year.

That was the first time I felt terror take me by the throat. Next day I happened to meet Bertha von Suttner, the generous and magnificent Cassandra of our times. An aristocrat from one of the first families in the land, in her early youth she had seen the horrors of the Austro-Prussian War of 1866 come close to their hereditary castle in Bohemia. With the passion of a Florence Nightingale, she saw only one task in life for herself—preventing a second war, preventing war in general. She wrote a novel entitled *Die Waffen nieder*—Lay Down Your Arms—which was an international success; she organised countless pacifist meetings, and the great triumph of her life was that she aroused the conscience of Alfred Nobel, the inventor of dynamite. He was induced to make up for the damage his invention had done by setting up the Nobel Peace Prize to foster international understanding. She came towards me in a state of great agitation. "People don't realise what's going on," she cried out loud in the street, although she usually spoke in quiet, kindly and composed tones. War was so close, and they were hiding everything from us and keeping it secret as usual. "Why don't you young people do something? It's more your business than anyone's! Resist, close ranks! Don't keep leaving everything to a few old women like us. No one listens to us!"

I told her that I was going to Paris, and perhaps we could try to draw up a joint manifesto there.

"Why 'perhaps'?" she urged me. "Things look worse than ever, the wheels have begun turning." Uneasy as I was myself, I had difficulty in calming her down.

But it was in France that a second, personal episode was to remind me how prophetically the old lady, who was not taken very seriously in Vienna, had foreseen the future. It was a very small incident, but it made a powerful impression on me. In the spring of 1914 I had left Paris, with a woman friend, to spend a few days in Touraine, where we were going to see the grave of Leonardo da Vinci. We had walked along the banks of the Loire in mild, sunny weather, and were pleasantly weary by evening. So we decided to go to the cinema in the rather sleepy town of Tours, where I had already paid my respects to the house in which Balzac was born.

It was a small suburban cinema, not at all like our modern picture palaces made of chromium and shining glass. Only a hall perfunctorily adapted for the purpose, and full of labourers, soldiers, market women, a crowd of ordinary people enjoying a gossip and blowing clouds of Scaferlati and Caporal tobacco smoke into the air, in defiance of a No Smoking sign. First on the screen came a newsreel—'News From All Over the World'. A boat race in England; the people talked and laughed. Then a French military parade, and again the audience took little notice. But the third item was entitled: 'Kaiser Wilhelm Visits Emperor Franz Joseph in Vienna'. Suddenly I saw on the screen the familiar platform of the Westbahnhof in Vienna, an ugly railway station building, along with a few policemen waiting for the train to come in. Then a signal was given, and old Emperor Franz Joseph walked past the guard of honour to welcome his guest. As the old Emperor appeared on the screen, stooping slightly and not entirely steady on his feet as he passed the line of men, the audience in Tours smiled kindly at the old gentleman with his white side whiskers. Then there was a picture of the train coming in, the first, the second and the third carriages. The door of the saloon car was opened, and out stepped Wilhelm II, the ends of his moustache bristling, wearing the uniform of an Austrian general.

At the moment when Kaiser Wilhelm appeared in the picture a storm of whistling and stamping broke out entirely spontaneously in the dark hall. Everyone was shouting and whistling, men, women and children all jeering as if they had been personally insulted. For a second the kindly people of Tours, who knew nothing about the world beyond what was in their newspapers, were out of their minds. I was horrified, deeply horrified. For I felt how far the poisoning of minds must have gone, after years and years of hate propaganda, if even here in a small provincial city the guileless citizens and soldiers had been roused to fury against the Kaiser and Germany—such fury that even a brief glimpse on the screen could provoke such an outburst. It was only a second, a single second. All was forgotten once other pictures were shown. The audience laughed heartily at the comedy that now followed, slapping their knees loudly with delight. Only a second, yes, but it showed me how easy it could be to whip up bad feeling on both sides at a moment of serious crisis, in spite of all attempts to restore understanding, in spite of our own efforts.

The entire evening was spoilt for me. I couldn't sleep. If it had happened in Paris, it would have made me just as uneasy, but it would not have shaken me so much. However, seeing how far hatred had eaten into the kindly, simple people here in the depths of the provinces made me shudder. In the next few days I told the story of this episode to many friends. Most of them didn't take it seriously. "Remember how we French mocked stout old Queen Victoria, and two years later came the Entente Cordiale with Britain. You don't know the French; they don't feel deeply about politics." Only Rolland saw it in a different light. "The simpler the people, the easier it is to win them over. Things have looked bad since Poincaré was elected. His journey to Petersburg will not be a pleasure jaunt." We talked for a long time about the International Socialist Congress that had been fixed for that summer in Vienna, but here too Rolland was more sceptical than most. "Who knows how many will stand firm once the posters ordering mobilisation go up? We have entered a time of mass emotion, crowd hysteria, and we cannot see yet what power it will have if war comes."

But, as I said earlier, such moments of anxiety passed by like gossamer blowing in the wind. We did think of war now and then, but in much the same way as one sometimes thinks of death—a possibility but probably far away. And Paris was too beautiful at that time, and we ourselves too young and happy to think of it much. I still remember a delightfully farcical ceremony devised by Jules Romains in which the idea of a *prince des poètes* was to be superseded by the crowning of a *prince des penseurs*, a good if rather simple-minded man who let the students lead him to the statue of Rodin's *Thinker* outside the Panthéon. In the evening we made merry like schoolboys at a parody of a banquet. The trees were in blossom, the air was sweet and mild; who wanted to think of something as unimaginable as war in the face of so many pleasures?

My friends were more my friends than ever, and I was making new friends too in a foreign land—an 'enemy' land. The city was more carefree than ever before, and we loved its freedom from care along with our own. In those final days I went with Verhaeren to Rouen, where he was to give a reading. That night we stood outside the cathedral, its spires gleaming magically in the moonlight—did such mild miracles belong to only one fatherland, didn't they belong to us all? At Rouen station, where one of the railway engines he had celebrated in verse was to crush him two years later,[7] we said our goodbyes. Verhaeren embraced me. "I'll see you on the first of August at Caillou qui Bique!" I promised to be there. I visited him at his place in the country every year to translate his new poems, working in close collaboration with him, so why not this year too? I said goodbye to my other friends without a care, goodbye to Paris, an unsentimental goodbye such as you say to your own house when you are just going away for a few weeks. My plan for the next few months was clear. I was off to Austria, to somewhere secluded in the country to get on with my work on Dostoevsky (which as things turned out could not be published until five years later), and thus complete my book on *Three Masters of Their Destiny*, depicting three great nations through the work of their greatest novelists. Then I would visit Verhaeren, and perhaps make my long-planned journey to Russia in winter, to form a group there as part of our movement for intellectual understanding. All lay plain and clear before me in this, my thirty-second year; that radiant summer the world offered itself like a delicious fruit. And I loved it for the sake of what it was now, and what it would be in an even greater future.

Then, on 28th June 1914, a shot was fired in Sarajevo, the shot that in a single second was to shatter the world of security and creative reason in which we had been reared, where we had grown up and were at home, as if it were a hollow clay pot breaking into a thousand pieces.

NOTES

1   This Zeppelin was the fourth model of the rigid airships developed
    by Count Ferdinand von Zeppelin through the last years of the nine-
    teenth century; the first took to the air in 1900. The one described
    by Zweig, LZ 4, landed at Echterdingen near Stuttgart in 1906 to
    satisfy the requirements of the German army, which was thinking
    of buying it. But it then tore away from its moorings in the air and
    was wrecked. Luckily there was no one inside it at the time.

2   Cyrenaica, a region of modern Libya occupied by Italy in 1911.

3   René Arcos, 1881-1959, French poet and novelist.

4   *The Market in the Square*, the subtitle of the first of Romain Rolland's
    ten novels in the *Jean-Christophe* series. It was published in 1908.

5   The magazine in which Rolland's *Jean-Christophe* novels were first
    published in serial form.

6   Also known as the Saverne Affair, from Saverne (in German Zabern)
    in Alsace, where incidents illustrating Prussian militarism foreshad-
    owed the Great War.

7   Emile Verhaeren was run over by a train and died at Rouen station
    in 1916.

From

BEWARE OF PITY

AUTHOR'S NOTE

A SHORT EXPLANATION may perhaps be necessary for the English reader. The Austro-Hungarian Army constituted a uniform, homogeneous body in an Empire composed of a very large number of nations and races. Unlike his English, French, and even German *confrère*, the Austrian officer was not allowed to wear mufti when off duty, and military regulations prescribed that in his private life he should always act *standesgemäss*, that is, in accordance with the special etiquette and code of honour of the Austrian military caste. Among themselves officers of the same rank, even those who were not personally acquainted, never addressed each other in the formal third person plural, *Sie*, but in the familiar second person singular, *Du*, and thereby the fraternity of all members of the caste and the gulf separating them from civilians were emphasised. The final criterion of an officer's behaviour was invariably not the moral code of society in general, but the special moral code of his caste, and this frequently led to mental conflicts, one of which plays an important part in this book.

STEFAN ZWEIG

INTRODUCTION

"To him that hath, more shall be given." Every writer knows the truth of this biblical maxim, and can confirm the fact that "To him who hath told much, more shall be told." There is nothing more erroneous than the idea, which is only too common, that a writer's imagination is always at work, and he is constantly inventing an inexhaustible supply of incidents and stories. In reality he does not have to invent his stories; he need only let characters and events find their own way to him, and if he retains to a high degree the ability to look and listen, they will keep seeking him out as someone who will pass them on. To him who has often tried to interpret the tales of others, many will tell their tales.

The incidents that follow were told to me almost entirely as I record them here, and in a wholly unexpected way. Last time I was in Vienna I felt tired after dealing with a great deal of business, and I went one evening to a suburban restaurant that I suspected had fallen out of fashion long ago, and would not be very full. As soon as I had come in, however, I found to my annoyance that I was wrong. An acquaintance of mine rose from the very first table with every evidence of high delight, to which I am afraid I could not respond quite so warmly, and asked me to sit down with him. It would not be true to say that this excessively friendly gentleman was disagreeable company in himself; but he was one of those compulsively sociable people who collect acquaintances as enthusiastically as children collect stamps, and like to show off every item in their collection. For this well-meaning oddity—a knowledgeable and competent archivist by profession—the whole meaning of life was confined to the modest satisfaction of being able to boast, in an offhand manner, of anyone whose name appeared in the newspapers from time to time, "Ah, he's a good friend of mine," or, "Oh, I met him only yesterday," or, "My friend A told me, and then my friend B gave it as his opinion that…" and so on all through the alphabet. He was regularly in the audience to applaud the premieres of his friends' plays, and would telephone every leading actress next morning with his congratulations, he never forgot a birthday, he never referred to any poor reviews of your work in the papers, but sent you those that praised it to the skies. Not a disagreeable man, then—his warmth of feeling was genuine, and he was delighted if you ever did him a small favour, or even added a new item to his fine collection of acquaintances.

However, there is no need for me to say more about my friend the hanger-on—such was the usual name in Vienna for this particular kind of well-intentioned parasite among the motley group of social climbers—for we all know hangers-on, and we also know that there is no way of repelling their well-meant attentions without being rude. So I resigned myself to sitting down beside him, and half-an-hour had passed in idle chatter when a man came into the restaurant. He was tall, his fresh-complexioned, still youthful face and the interesting touch of grey at his temples made him a striking figure, and a certain way of holding himself very upright marked him out at once as a former military man. My table companion immediately leapt to his feet with a typically warm greeting, to which, however, the gentleman responded with more indifference than civility, and the newcomer had hardly ordered from the attentive waiter who came hurrying up before my friend the lion-hunter was leaning towards me and asking in a whisper, "Do you know who that is?" As I well knew his collector's pride in displaying his collection, and I feared a lengthy story, I said only a brief, "No," and went back to dissecting my

Sachertorte. However, my lack of interest only aroused further enthusiasm in the collector of famous names, and he confidentially whispered, "Why, that's Hofmiller of the General Commissariat—you know, the man who won the Order of Maria Theresia in the war." And since even this did not seem to impress me as much as he had hoped, he launched with all the enthusiasm of a patriotic textbook into an account of the great achieve-ments of this Captain Hofmiller, first in the cavalry, then on the famous reconnaissance flight over the river Piave when he shot down three enemy aircraft single-handed, and finally the time when he occupied and held a sector of the front for three days with his company of gunners—all with a wealth of detail that I omit here, and many expressions of astonishment at finding that I had never heard of this great man, decorated by Emperor Karl in person with the highest order in the Austrian Army.

Reluctantly, I let myself be persuaded to glance at the other table for a closer view of a historically authentic hero. But I met with a look of annoyance, as much as to say—has that fellow been talking about me? There's no need to stare! At the same time the gentleman pushed his chair to one side with an air of distinct displeasure, ostentatiously turning his back to us. Feeling a little ashamed of myself, I looked away from him, and from then on I avoided looking curiously at anything, even the tablecloth. Soon after that I said goodbye to my talkative friend. I noticed as I left that he immediately moved to the table where his military hero was sitting, probably to give him an account of me as eagerly as he had talked to me about Hofmiller.

That was all. A mere couple of glances, and I would certainly have forgotten that brief meeting, but at a small party the very next day it so happened that I again found myself opposite the same unsociable gentle-man, who incidentally looked even more striking and elegant in a dinner jacket than he had in his casual tweeds the day before. We both had some difficulty in suppressing a small smile, the kind exchanged in a company of any size by two people who share a well-kept secret. He recognised me as easily as I did him, and probably we felt the same amusement in thinking of the mutual acquaintance who had failed to throw us together yesterday. At first we avoided speaking to one another, and indeed there was not much chance to do so, because an animated discussion was going on around us.

I shall be giving away the subject of that discussion in advance if I mention that it took place in the year 1938. Later historians of our time will agree that in 1938 almost every conversation, in every country of our ruined continent of Europe, revolved around the probability or otherwise of a second world war. The theme inevitably fascinated every social gathering, and you sometimes felt that fears, suppositions and hopes were being expressed not so much by the speakers as by the atmosphere itself, the air of those times, highly charged with secret tensions and anxious to put them into words.

The subject had been broached by the master of the house, a lawyer and self-opinionated, as lawyers tend to be. He trotted out the usual arguments to prove the usual nonsense—the younger generation knew about war now, he said, and would not stumble blindly into another one. At the moment of mobilisation, guns would be turned on those who had given orders to fire them. Men like him in particular, said our host, men who had fought at the front in the last war, had not forgotten what it was like. At a time when explosives and poison gas were being manufactured in tens of thousands—no, hundreds of thousands—of armaments factories, he dismissed the possibility of war as easily as he flicked the ash off his cigarette, speaking in a confident tone that irritated me. We shouldn't always, I firmly retorted, believe in our own wishful thinking. The civil and military organisations directing the apparatus of war had not been asleep, and while our heads were spinning with utopian notions they had made the maximum use of peacetime to get control of the population at large. It had been organised in advance and was now, so to speak, primed ready to fire. Even now, thanks to our sophisticated propaganda machine, general subservience had grown to extraordinary proportions, and we had only to look facts in the face to see that when mobilisation was announced on the radio sets in our living rooms, no resistance could be expected. Men today were just motes of dust with no will of their own left.

Of course everyone else was against me. We all know from experience how the human tendency to self-delusion likes to declare dangers null and void even when we sense in our hearts that they are real. And such a warning against cheap optimism was certain to be unwelcome at the magnificently laid supper table in the next room.

Unexpectedly, although I had assumed that the hero who had won the Order of Maria Theresia would be an adversary, he now spoke up and took my side. It was sheer nonsense, he said firmly, to suppose that what ordinary people wanted or did not want counted for anything today. In the next war machinery would do the real work, and human beings would be downgraded to the status of machine parts. Even in the last war, he said, he had not met many men in the field who were clearly either for or against it. Most of them had been caught up in hostilities like a cloud of dust in the wind, and there they were, stuck in the whirl of events, shaken about and helpless like dried peas in a big bag. All things considered, he said, perhaps more men had fled into the war than away from it.

I listened in surprise, particularly interested by the vehemence with which he went on. "Let's not delude ourselves. If you were to try drumming up support in any country today for a war in a completely different part of the world, say Polynesia or some remote corner of Africa, thousands and tens of thousands would volunteer as recruits without really knowing *why, perhaps just out of a desire to get away from themselves or their unsatisfactory lives. But I can't put the chances of any real opposition to the idea of war higher than zero. It takes far more courage for a man to oppose an organisation than to go along with the crowd. Standing up to it calls for individualism, and individualists are a dying species in these times of progressive organisation and mechanisation. In the war the instances of courage that I met could be called courage en masse, courage within the ranks, and if you look closely at that phenomenon you'll find some very strange elements in it—a good deal of vanity, thoughtlessness, even boredom, but mainly fear—fear of lagging behind, fear of mockery, fear of taking independent action, and most of all fear of opposing the united opinion of your companions. Most of those whom I knew on the field as the bravest of the brave seemed to me very dubious heroes when I returned to civil life. And please don't misunderstand me," he added, turning courteously to our host, who had a wry look on his face, "I make no exception at all for myself."*

I liked the way he spoke, and would have gone over for a word with him, but just then the lady of the house summoned us to supper, and as we were seated some way apart we had no chance to talk. Only when everyone was leaving did we meet in the cloakroom.

"I think," he said to me, with a smile, "that we've already been introduced by our mutual friend."

I smiled back. "And at such length, too."

"I expect he laid it on thick, presenting me as an Achilles and carrying on about my order."

"Something like that."

"Yes, he's very proud of my order—and of your books as well."

"An oddity, isn't he? Still, there are worse. Shall we walk a little way together?"

As we were leaving, he suddenly turned to me. "Believe me, I mean it when I tell you that over the years the Order of Maria Theresia has been nothing but a nuisance to me. Too showy by half for my liking. Although to be honest, when it was handed out to me on the battlefield of course I was delighted at first. After all, when you've been trained as a soldier and from your days at military academy on you've heard about the legendary order—it's given to perhaps only a dozen men in any war—well, it's like a star falling from heaven into your lap. A thing like that means a lot to a young man of twenty-eight. All of a sudden there you are in front of everyone, they're all staring at something shining on your chest like a little sun, and the Emperor himself, His Unapproachable Majesty, is shaking your hand and congratulating you. But you see, it's a distinction that meant nothing outside the world of the army, and after the war it struck me as ridiculous to be going around as a certified hero for the rest of my life, just because I'd shown real courage for twenty minutes—probably no more courage, in fact, than ten thousand others. All that distinguished me from them was that I had attracted attention and, perhaps even more surprising, I'd come back alive. After a year when everyone stared at that little bit of metal, with their eyes wandering over me in awe, I felt sick and tired of going around like a monument on the move, and I hated all the fuss. That's one of the reasons why I switched to civilian life so soon after the end of the war."

He began walking a little faster.

"One of the reasons, I said, but the main reason was private, and you may find it easier to understand. The main reason was that I had grave doubts of my right to be decorated at all, or at least of my heroism. I knew better than any of the gaping strangers that behind that order was a man who was far from being a hero, was even decidedly a non-hero—one of those who ran full tilt into the war to save themselves from a desperate *situation. Deserters from their own responsibilities, not heroes doing their duty. I don't know how it seems to you, but I for one see life lived in an aura of heroism as unnatural and unbearable, and I felt genuinely relieved when I could give up parading my heroic story on my uniform for all to see. It still irritates me to hear someone digging up the old days of my glory, and I might as well admit that yesterday I was on the point of going over to your table and telling our loquacious friend, in no uncertain terms, to boast of knowing someone else, not me. Your look of respect rankled, and I felt like showing how wrong our friend was by making you listen to the tale of the devious ways whereby I acquired my heroic reputation. It's a very strange story, and it certainly shows that courage is often only another aspect of weakness. Incidentally, I would still have no reservations about telling you that tale. What happened to a man a quarter-of-a-century ago no longer concerns him personally—it happened to someone different. Do you have the time and inclination to hear it?"*

Of course I had time, and we walked up and down the now deserted streets for some while longer. In the following days, we also spent a great deal of time together. I have changed very little in Captain Hofmiller's account, at most making a regiment of hussars into a regiment of lancers, moving garrisons around the map a little to hide their identity, and carefully changing all the personal names. But I have not added anything of importance, and it is not I as the writer of this story but its real narrator who now begins to tell his tale.

T HE WHOLE AFFAIR BEGAN with a piece of ineptitude, of entirely accidental foolishness, a faux pas, as the French would say. Next came my attempt to make up for my stupidity. But if you try to repair a little cogwheel in clockwork too quickly, you can easily ruin the whole mechanism. Even today, years later, I don't know exactly where plain clumsiness ended and my own guilt began. Presumably I never shall.

I was twenty-five years old at the time, a lieutenant serving in a regiment of lancers. I can't say that I ever felt any particular enthusiasm for the career of an army officer, or a special vocation for it. But when an old Austrian family with a tradition of service to the state has two girls and four boys, all with hearty appetites, sitting around a sparsely laid table, no one stops for long to consider the young people's own inclinations. They are put through the mill of training for some profession early, to keep them from being a burden on the household. My brother Ulrich, who had ruined his eyesight with too much studying even at elementary school, was sent to a seminar for the priesthood, while I, being physically strong and sturdy, entered the military academy. From such chance beginnings the course of your life moves automatically on, and you don't even have to oil the wheels. The state takes care of everything. Within a few years, working to a preordained pattern, it makes a pale adolescent boy into an ensign with a downy beard on his chin, and hands him over to the army ready for use. I passed out from the academy on the Emperor's birthday, when I was not quite eighteen years old, and soon after that I had my first star on my collar. I had reached the first stage of a military career, and now the cycle of promotion could move automatically on at suitable intervals until I reached retirement age and had gout. I was to serve in the cavalry, unfortunately an expensive section of the army, not by any wish of my own but because of a whim on the part of my aunt Daisy, my father's elder brother's second wife. They had married when he moved from the Ministry of Finance to a more profitable post as managing director of a bank. Aunt Daisy, who was both rich and a snob, could not bear to think that anyone who happened to be called Hofmiller should bring the family name into disrepute by serving in the infantry, and as she could afford to indulge her whim by making me an allowance of a hundred crowns a month, I had to express my humble gratitude to her at every opportunity. No one, least of all I myself, had ever stopped to wonder whether I would enjoy life in a cavalry regiment, or indeed any kind of military service. But once in the saddle I felt at ease, and I didn't think much further ahead than my horse's neck.

In that November of 1913, some kind of decree must have passed from office to office, because all of a sudden my squadron had been transferred from Jaroslav to another small garrison on the Hungarian border. It makes no difference whether I give the little town its real name or not, for two uniform buttons on the same coat can't be more like each other than one provincial Austrian garrison town is to another. You

find the same ubiquitous features in both: a barracks, a riding
school, a parade ground, an officers' mess, and the town will
have three hotels, two cafés, a cake shop, a bar, a run-down
music hall with faded soubrettes whose professional sideline
consists of dividing their affections between the regular officers
and volunteers who have joined up for a year. Army service
means the same sleepy, empty monotony everywhere, divided
up hour by hour according to the old iron rules, and even
an officer's leisure time offers little more variety. You see the
same faces and conduct the same conversations in the officers' mess, you play the same card games and the same games
of billiards in the café. Sometimes you are quite surprised
that it has at least pleased the Almighty to set the six to eight
hundred rooftops of these small towns under different skies
and in different landscapes.

But my new garrison did have one advantage over my earlier
posting in Galicia—a railway station where express trains
stopped. Go one way and it was quite close to Vienna, go the
other and it was not too far from Budapest. A man who had
money—and everyone who served in the cavalry was rich, even
and indeed not least the volunteers, some of them members
of the great aristocracy, others manufacturers' sons—a man
who had money could, with careful planning, go to Vienna
on the five o'clock train and return on the night train, getting
in at two-thirty next morning. That gave him time for a visit
to the theatre and a stroll around the Ringstrasse, courting
the ladies and sometimes going in search of a little adventure.
Some of the most envied officers even kept a permanent
apartment for a mistress in Vienna, or a pied-à-terre. But

such refreshing diversions were more than I could afford on my monthly allowance. My only entertainment was going to the café or the cake shop, and since cards were usually played for stakes too high for me, I resorted to those establishments to play billiards—or chess, which was even cheaper.

So one afternoon—it must have been in the middle of May 1914—I was sitting in the cake shop with one of my occasional partners, the pharmacist who kept his shop at the sign of the Golden Eagle, and who was also deputy mayor of our little garrison town. We had long ago finished playing our usual three games, and were just talking idly about this or that—what was there in this tedious place to make you want to get up in the morning?—but the conversation was drowsy, and as slow as the smoke from a cigarette burning down.

At this point the door suddenly opens, and a pretty girl in a full-skirted dress is swept in on a gust of fresh air, a girl with brown, almond-shaped eyes and a dark complexion. She is dressed with real elegance, not at all in the provincial style. Above all she is a new face in the monotony of this godforsaken town. Sad to say, the elegantly dressed young lady does not spare us a glance as we respectfully admire her, but walks briskly and vivaciously with a firm, athletic gait past the nine little marble tables in the cake shop and up to the sales counter, to order cakes, tarts and liqueurs by the dozen. I immediately notice how respectfully the master confectioner bows to her—I've never seen the back seam of his swallow-tailed coat stretched so taut. Even his wife, that opulent if heavily built provincial Venus, who in the usual way negligently allows the officers to court her (all manner of little things often go unpaid for until the end of the month), rises from her seat at the cash desk and almost dissolves in obsequious civilities. While the master confectioner notes down the order in the customers' book, the pretty girl carelessly nibbles a couple of chocolates and makes a little conversation with Frau Grossmaier. However, she has no time to spare for us, and we may perhaps be craning our necks with unbecoming alacrity. Of course the young lady does not burden her own pretty hands with a single package; everything, as Frau Grossmaier assures her, will be delivered, she can rely on that. Nor does she think for a moment of paying cash at the till, as we mere mortals must. We all know at once that this is a very superior and distinguished customer.

Now, as she turns to go after leaving her order, Herr Grossmaier hastily leaps forward to open the door for her. My friend the pharmacist also rises from his chair to offer his respectful greetings as she floats past. She thanks him with gracious friendliness—heavens, what velvety brown eyes, the colour of a roe deer—and I can hardly wait until she has left the shop, amidst many fulsome compliments, to ask my chess partner with great interest about this girl, a pike in a pond full of fat carp.

"Oh, don't you know her? Why, she is the niece of … "—well, I will call him Herr von Kekesfalva, although that was not really the name—"she is the niece of Herr von Kekesfalva—surely you know the Kekesfalvas?"

Kekesfalva—he throws out the name as if it were a thousand-crown note, and looks at me as if expecting a respectful "Ah yes! Of course!" as the right and proper echo of his information. But I, a young lieutenant transferred to my new garrison only a few months ago, and unsuspecting as I am, know nothing about that mysterious luminary, and ask politely for further enlightenment, which the pharmacist gives with all the satisfaction of provincial pride, and it goes without saying does so at far greater length and with more loquacity than I do in recording his information here.

Kekesfalva, he explains to me, is the richest man in the whole district. Absolutely everything belongs to him, not just Kekesfalva Castle—"You must know the castle, it can be seen from the parade ground, it's over to the left of the road, the yellow castle with the low tower and the large old park." Kekesfalva also owns the big sugar factory on the road to R, the sawmill in Bruck and the stud farm in M. They are all his property, as well as six or seven apartment blocks in Vienna and Budapest. "You might not think that we had such wealthy folk here, but he lives the life of a real magnate. In winter, he goes to his little Viennese palace in Jacquingasse, in summer he visits spa resorts, he stays at home here only for a few months in spring, but heavens above, what a household he keeps! Visiting quartets from Vienna, champagne and French wines, the best of everything!" And if it would interest me, says the pharmacist, he will be happy to take me to the castle, for—here he makes a grand gesture of self-satisfaction—he is on friendly terms with Herr von Kekesfalva, has often done business with him in the past, and knows that he is always glad to welcome army officers to his house. My chess partner has only to say the word, and I'll be invited.

Well, why not? Here I am, stifling in the dreary backwaters of a provincial garrison town. I already know every one of the women who go walking on the promenade in the evenings by sight, I know their summer hats and winter hats, their Sunday best and their everyday dresses, always the same. And from looking and then looking away again, I know these ladies' dogs and their maidservants and their children. I know all the culinary skills of the stout Bohemian woman who is cook in the officers' mess, and by now a glance at the menu in the restaurant, which like the meals in the mess is always the same, quite takes away my appetite. I know every name, every shop sign, every poster in every street by heart, I know which business has premises in which building, and which shop will have what on display in its window. I know almost as well as Eugen the head waiter the time at which the district judge will come into the café, I know he will sit down at the corner by the window on the left, to order a Viennese melange, while the local notary will arrive exactly ten minutes later, at four-forty, and will drink lemon tea for the sake of his weak stomach—what a daring change from coffee!—while telling the same jokes as he smokes the same Virginia cigarette. Yes, I know all the faces, all the uniforms, all the horses and all the drivers, all the beggars in the entire neighbourhood, and I know myself better than I like! So why not get off this treadmill for once? And then there's that pretty girl with her warm, brown eyes. So I tell my acquaintance, pretending to be indifferent (I don't want to seem too keen in front of that conceited pill-roller) that yes, it would be a pleasure to meet the Kekesfalva family.

Sure enough—for my friend the pharmacist was not just showing off—two days later, puffed up with pride, he brings a printed card to the café with my name entered on it in an elegant calligraphic hand and gives it to me with a flourish. On this invitation card, Herr Lajos von Kekesfalva requests the pleasure of the company of Lieutenant Anton Hofmiller at dinner on Wednesday next week, at eight in the evening. Thank Heaven, I am not of such humble origins that I don't know the way to behave in these circumstances. On Sunday morning, dressed in my best, white gloves, patent leather shoes, meticulously shaved, a drop of eau de cologne on my moustache, I drive out to pay a courtesy call. The manservant—old, discreet, good livery—takes my card and murmurs, apologetically, that the family will be very sorry to have missed seeing Lieutenant Hofmiller, but they are at church. All the better, I tell myself, courtesy calls are always a terrible bore. Anyway, I've done my duty. On Wednesday evening, I tell myself, you'll go off there again, and it's to be hoped the occasion will be pleasant. That's the Kekesfalva affair dealt with until Wednesday. Two days later, however, on Tuesday, I am genuinely pleased to find a visiting card from Herr von Kekesfalva handed in for me, with one corner of it turned down. Good, I think, these people have perfect manners. A general could hardly have been shown more civility and respect than Herr von Kekesfalva has paid me, an insignificant officer, by returning my original courtesy call two days later. And I begin looking forward to Wednesday evening with real pleasure.

But there's a hitch at the very start—I suppose one should be superstitious and pay more attention to small signs and omens. There I am at seven-thirty on Wednesday evening, ready in my best uniform, new gloves, patent leather shoes, creases in my trousers ironed straight as a knife blade, and my batman is adjusting the folds of my overcoat and checking the general effect (I always need him to do that, because I have only a small hand mirror in my poorly lit room), when an orderly knocks vigorously on the door. The duty officer, my friend Captain Count Steinhübel, wants me to go over to join him in the guardroom. Two lancers, probably as drunk as lords, have been quarrelling, and it ended with one hitting the other over the head with the stock of his rifle. Now the idiot who suffered the blow is lying there bleeding and unconscious, with his mouth open. No one knows whether or not his skull is intact. The regimental doctor has gone to Vienna on leave, the Colonel can't be found, so Steinhübel summons me to help him in his hour of need, damn his eyes. While he sees to the injured man, I have to write a report on the incident and send orderlies all over the place to drum up a civilian doctor from the café or wherever there's one to be found. By now it is a quarter to eight, and I can see that there's no chance of my getting away for another fifteen minutes or half-an-hour. Why in Heaven's name does this have to happen today of all days, when I'm invited out to dinner? Feeling more and more impatient, I look at the time. Even if I have to hang around here for only another five minutes, I can't possibly arrive punctually. But the principle that military service takes precedence over any private engagement has been dinned into us. I can't get out of it, so I do the only possible thing in this stupid situation, I send my batman off in a cab (which costs me four crowns) to the Kekesfalva house, to deliver my apologies in case I am late, explaining that an unexpected incident at the barracks… and so on and so forth. Fortunately the commotion at the barracks doesn't last long, because the Colonel arrives in person with a doctor found in haste, and now I can slip inconspicuously away.

Bad luck again, however—there's no cab in the square outside the town hall, I have to wait while someone telephones for a two-horse carriage. So it's inevitable, when I finally arrive in the hall of Herr von Kekesfalva's house, that the big hand of the clock on the wall is pointing vertically down; it is eight-thirty instead of eight, and the coats in the cloakroom are piled on top of each other. The rather anxious look on the servant's face also shows me that I am decidedly late—how unlucky, how really unlucky for such a thing to happen on a first visit.

However, the servant—this time in white gloves, tailcoat and a starched shirt to go with his starchy expression—reassures me; my batman delivered my message half-an-hour ago, he says, and he leads me into the salon, four windows curtained in red silk, the room sparkling with light from crystal chandeliers, fabulously elegant, I've never seen anywhere more splendid. But to my dismay it is deserted, and I clearly hear the cheerful clink of plates in the room next to it—how very annoying, I think at once, they've already started dinner!

Well, I pull myself together, and as soon as the servant pushes the double door open ahead of me I step into the dining room, click my heels smartly, and bow. Everyone looks up, twenty, forty eyes, all of them the eyes of strangers, inspect the late-comer standing there by the doorpost feeling very unsure of himself. An elderly gentleman is already rising from his chair, undoubtedly the master of the house, quickly putting down his napkin. He comes towards me and welcomes me, offering me his hand. Herr von Kekesfalva does not look at all as I imagined him, not in the least like a landed nobleman, no flamboyant Magyar moustache, full cheeks, stout and red-faced from good wine. Instead, rather weary eyes with grey bags under them swim behind gold-rimmed glasses, he has something of a stoop, his voice is a whisper slightly impeded by coughing. With his thin, delicately featured face, ending in a sparse, pointed white beard, you would be more likely to take him for a scholar. The old man's marked kindness is immensely reassuring to me in my uncertainty; no, no, he interrupts me at once, it is for him to apologise. He knows just how it is, anything can happen when you're on army service, and it was particularly good of me to let him know; they had begun dinner only because they couldn't be sure whether I would arrive at all. But now I must sit down at once. He will introduce me to all the company individually after dinner. Except that here—and he leads me to the table—this is his daughter. A girl in her teens, delicate, pale, as fragile as her father, looks up from a conversation, and two grey eyes shyly rest on me. But I see her thin, nervous face only in passing, I bow first to her, then right and left to the company in general, who are obviously glad not to have to lay down their knives and forks and have the meal interrupted by formal introductions.

For the first two or three minutes I still feel very uncomfortable. There's no one else from the regiment here, none of my comrades, no one I know, not even any of the more prominent citizens of the little town, all the guests are total strangers to me. Most of them seem to be the owners of nearby estates with their wives and daughters, some are civil servants. But they are all civilians; mine is the only uniform. My God, clumsy and shy as I am, how am I going to make conversation with these unknown people? Fortunately I've been well placed. Next to me sits that brown, high-spirited girl, the pretty niece, who seems to have noticed my admiring glance in the cake shop after all, for she gives me a friendly smile as if I were an old acquaintance. She has eyes like coffee beans, and indeed when she laughs it's with a softly sizzling sound like coffee beans roasting. She has enchanting, translucent little ears under her thick black hair, ears like pink cyclamen flowers growing in dark moss, I think. Her bare arms are soft and smooth; they must feel like peaches.

It does me good to be sitting next to such a pretty girl, and her Hungarian accent when she speaks almost has me falling in love with her. It does me good to eat at such an elegantly laid table in so bright and sparkling a room, with liveried servants behind me and the finest dishes in front of me. My neighbour on the left speaks with a slight Polish accent, and although she is built rather on the generous scale she too seems to me a very attractive sight. Or is that just the effect of the wine, pale gold, then dark red, and now the bubbles of champagne, poured unstintingly from silver carafes by the servants with their white gloves standing behind us? No, the good pharmacist was not exaggerating. You might think yourself at court in the Kekesfalva house. I have never eaten so well, or even dreamt that anyone *could* eat so well, so lavishly, could taste such delicacies. More and more exquisite dishes are carried in on inexhaustible platters, blue-tinged fish crowned with lettuce and framed by slices of lobster swim in golden sauces, capons ride aloft on broad saddles of piled rice, puddings are flambéed in rum, burning with a blue flame; ice bombs fall apart to reveal their sweet, colourful contents, fruits that must have travelled halfway round the world nestle close to each other in silver baskets. It never, never ends, and finally there is a positive rainbow of liqueurs, green, red, colourless, yellow, and cigars as thick as asparagus, to be enjoyed with delicious coffee!

A wonderful, a magical house—blessings on the good pharmacist!—a bright, happy evening full of merry sound! Do I feel so relaxed, so much at ease, just because the eyes of the other guests, to my right and my left and opposite me, are also shining now, and they have raised their voices? They too seem to have forgotten about etiquette and are talking nineteen to the dozen! Anyway, my own usual shyness is gone. I chatter on without the slightest inhibition, I pay court to both the ladies sitting next to me, I drink, laugh, look around in cheerful high spirits, and if it isn't always by chance that my hand now and then touches the lovely bare arm of Ilona (such is the name of the delectable niece), then she doesn't seem to take my gentle approach and then retreat in the wrong spirit, she is relaxed and elated like all of us at this lavish banquet.

I begin to feel—while wondering if it may not be the effect of the unusually good wine; Tokay and champagne in such quick succession?—I begin to feel elated, buoyant, even boisterous. I need only one thing to crown my happiness in the spell cast over my enraptured mind, and what I have unconsciously been wanting is revealed to me next moment, when I suddenly hear soft music, performed by a quartet of instrumentalists, beginning to play in a third room beyond the salon. The servant has quietly opened the double doors again. It is exactly the kind of music I would have wished for, dance music, rhythmical and gentle at the same time, a waltz with the melody played by two violins, the low notes of a cello adding a darker tone, and a piano picking out the tune in sharp staccato. Music, yes, music, that was all I still needed! Music now, and perhaps dancing, a waltz! I want to move with it, feel that I am flying, sense my lightness of heart even more blissfully! This Villa Kekesfalva must indeed be a magical place where you have only to dream of something and your wish is granted. So now we stand up, moving our dining chairs aside, and two by two—I offer Ilona my arm, and once again feel her cool, soft, beautiful skin—we go into the salon, where the tables have been cleared away as if by brownie magic, and chairs are placed around the wall. The wooden floor is smooth and shiny, a mirror-like brown surface, waltzing is the apotheosis of skating, and the lively music played by the invisible instrumentalist next door animates us.

I turn to Ilona. She laughs, understanding me. Her eyes have already said "Yes", and now we are whirling round the room, two couples, three couples, five couples moving over the whole dance floor, while the older and less daring guests watch or talk to each other. I like dancing, I may even say I dance well. Closely entwined, we skim the floor. I think I have never danced better in my life. I ask my other neighbour at dinner for the pleasure of the next waltz. She too dances very well, and leaning down to her I smell the perfume of her hair and feel slightly dizzy. Oh, her dancing is wonderful, it is all wonderful, I haven't felt so happy for years. I hardly know what I am doing, I would like to embrace everyone, say something heartfelt, grateful to them all, I feel so light, so elated, so blissfully young. I whirl from partner to partner, I talk and laugh and dance, and never notice the time, carried away by the torrent of my pleasure.

Then I suddenly look up and happen to see the time. It is ten-thirty—and I realise, to my alarm, that I have been dancing and talking and amusing myself for almost an hour but, great oaf that I am, I haven't yet asked my host's daughter to dance. I have only danced with my two neighbours at dinner and two or three other ladies, the ones I liked best, entirely neglecting the daughter of the house! What uncivil behaviour, what a slight to her! I must put that right at once!

I am shocked, however, to realise that I cannot remember exactly what the girl looks like. I bowed to her only briefly when she was already seated at table, all I recollect is the impression of fragile delicacy that she made on me, and then the quick, curious glance of her grey eyes. But where is she? She is the daughter of the house, surely she can't have left the party? I look uneasily at all the girls and women sitting by the wall; I see no one like her. Finally I step into the third room where, hidden behind a Japanese screen, the quartet is playing, and breathe a sigh of relief. For there she is—yes, I am sure of it—delicate, slender, sitting in her pale-blue dress between two old ladies in the corner of this boudoir, at a malachite-green table with a shallow bowl of flowers on it. Her head is slightly bowed, as if she were entirely absorbed in the music, and the deep crimson of the roses in the bowl makes me notice the translucent pallor of her forehead under her heavy light-red hair. But I have no time for idle gazing. Thank God, I think fervently, now I've tracked her down, and I can make up for being so remiss.

I go over to the table—the music is playing merrily away—and bow to indicate that I am asking her to dance. She looks at me in startled surprise, her lips still half open, interrupted in the middle of what she was saying. But she makes no move to rise and go with me. Didn't she understand? I bow again, and my spurs clink softly. "May I have the pleasure of this dance, dear young lady?"

Something terrible happens next. She had been leaning slightly forward, but now she flinches abruptly back as if avoiding a blow. At the same time the blood rushes into her pale cheeks, the lips that were half open just now are pressed hard together, and only her eyes keep staring at me with an expression of horror such as I have never seen in my life before. Next moment a paroxysm passes right through her convulsed body. She braces herself on the table with both hands, making the bowl of roses clink and jangle, and at the same time something hard, made of wood or metal, falls from her chair to the ground. Both her hands are still clutching the table, which sways, her childlike body is shaken again and again, but all the same she does not run away, she only clings even more desperately to the heavy tabletop. And again and again that shaking, those tremors run from her cramped fists all the way up to her hairline. Suddenly she bursts into sobs, a wild, elemental sound like a stifled scream.

But the two old ladies are already with her, to right and left, one on each side, holding her, caressing her, speaking soothing, reassuring words to the trembling girl. Her convulsed hands relax, drop gently from the table, and she falls back into her chair. However, the weeping goes on, even worse than before, like a rush of blood, like a surge of hot vomit rising in her throat it keeps bursting forth. If the music drowning the sound of it out from behind the screen were to stop for a moment, even the dancers in the next room would hear her sobbing.

I stand there, horrified, bewildered. What exactly has happened? Baffled, I stare at the two old ladies as they try to calm the sobbing girl. Now, as she begins to feel ashamed of her outburst, she has laid her head on the table. But she still breaks into fresh tears again and again, wave after wave of them shaking her slender body up to her shoulders, and each of these abrupt fits of weeping makes the glass and china clink. As for me, I stand there at a loss, my thoughts frozen like ice, with my collar constricting my throat like a burning cord.

"I'm sorry," I finally stammer in an undertone, and while both ladies are busy with the sobbing girl—neither of them spares me a glance—I retreat, feeling dizzy, into the hall beyond. No one here seems to have noticed anything yet. Couples are circling with verve on the dance floor, and I have to hold on to the doorpost, because the room is going round and round before my eyes. What happened? Have I done something wrong? My God, did I drink too much and too fast at dinner, did I drink enough to stupefy me and make me commit some silly blunder?

The music stops, the couples move apart. The district

administrator who is Ilona's partner relinquishes her hand with a bow, and I immediately hurry over to her and make the surprised girl go over to the window with me. "Please help me! For Heaven's sake, help me, explain!"

Obviously Ilona was expecting me to whisper something amusing to her when I took her aside, for suddenly her glance is unfriendly. I must have looked either pitiable or alarming in my agitation. My pulse beats fast as I tell her everything. And strange to say, she cries out with the same sheer horror in her eyes as the girl in the other room.

"Are you out of your mind?… Don't you know?… Didn't you notice?…"

"No," I stammer, shattered by these fresh and equally incomprehensible signs of horror. "Didn't I notice *what*? And I don't know anything—this is the first time I've been in this house."

"But didn't you see that Edith is… is lame? Didn't you notice her poor crippled legs? She can't drag herself two paces without crutches, and then you… you callous…" (here she quickly suppresses some angry term for me). "Then you ask the poor girl to dance… oh, how dreadful! I must go straight to her."

"No"—and in my desperation I clutch Ilona's arm—"just a moment, one moment… you must give her my apologies for everything. I couldn't guess… I'd only seen her sitting at the dinner table, just for a second… please explain that…"

But Ilona, with anger in her eyes, has already freed her arm and is on her way to the other room. I stand in the doorway of the salon, my throat tight, the taste of sickness in my mouth. All around me there is dancing, couples circling on the floor, chattering voices as the guests talk and laugh in a carefree way that is suddenly more than I can bear. Another five minutes, I think, and everyone will know about my folly. Five more minutes, and then scornful, disapproving, ironic glances will be cast at me from all sides, and tomorrow the story of my rough, clumsy behaviour, passed on by a hundred mouths, will be the talk of the whole town, delivered at back doors with the milk, retold in the servants' quarters, reaching the cafés and offices. Tomorrow my regiment will know about it.

At that moment, as if through a mist, I see the girl's father. He is crossing the salon with a rather anxious expression—does he know already? Is he on his way towards me? No—oh, if I can only avoid him now! I am suddenly in panic terror of him, of everyone. And without really knowing what I am doing, I stumble to the door leading into the front hall, and so out of this infernal house.

"Are you leaving us already, sir?" asks the surprised servant, with a look of respectful incredulity.

"Yes," I reply, and take fright to hear the word come out of my mouth. Do I really want to leave? Next moment, as he takes my coat off the hook where it is hanging, I realise that by running away now I am committing another stupid and perhaps even more unforgivable offence. However, it is too late to change my mind. I can't suddenly hand my coat back to the servant as he opens the front door for me with a little bow, I can't go back into the salon. And so there I am all of a sudden, standing outside that strange, that accursed house, with the cold wind in my face, hot shame in my heart, and breathing as convulsively as if I were being choked.

TWENTY-FOUR HOURS IN
THE LIFE OF A WOMAN

IN THE LITTLE GUEST HOUSE on the Riviera where I was staying at the time, ten years before the war, a heated discussion had broken out at our table and unexpectedly threatened to degenerate into frenzied argument, even rancour and recrimination. Most people have little imagination. If something doesn't affect them directly, does not drive a sharp wedge straight into their minds, it hardly excites them at all, but if an incident, however slight, takes place before their eyes, close enough for the senses to perceive it, it instantly rouses them to extremes of passion. They compensate for the infrequency of their sympathy, as it were, by exhibiting disproportionate and excessive vehemence.

Such was the case that day among our thoroughly bourgeois company at table, where on the whole we just made equable small talk and cracked mild little jokes, usually parting as soon as the meal was over: the German husband and wife to go on excursions and take snapshots, the portly Dane to set out on tedious fishing expeditions, the distinguished English lady to return to her books, the Italian married couple to indulge in escapades to Monte Carlo, and I to lounge in a garden chair or get some work done. This time, however, our irate discussion left us all still very much at odds, and if someone suddenly rose it was not, as usual, to take civil leave of the rest of us, but in a mood of heated irascibility that, as I have said, was assuming positively frenzied form.

The incident obsessing our little party, admittedly, was odd enough. From outside, the guest house where the seven of us were staying might have been an isolated villa—with a wonderful view of the rock-strewn beach from its windows—but in fact it was only the cheaper annexe of the Grand Palace Hotel to which it was directly linked by the garden, so that we in the guest house were in constant touch with the hotel guests. And that same hotel had been the scene of an outright scandal the day before, when a young Frenchman had arrived by the midday train, at twenty-past twelve (I can't avoid giving the time so precisely because it was of importance to the incident itself, and indeed to the subject of our agitated conversation), and took a room with a view of the sea, opening straight on to the beach, which in itself indicated that he was in reasonably easy circumstances. Not only his discreet elegance but, most of all, his extraordinary and very appealing good looks made an attractive impression. A silky blond moustache surrounded sensuously warm lips in a slender, girlish face; soft, wavy brown hair curled over his pale forehead; every glance of his melting eyes was a caress—indeed everything about him was soft, endearing, charming, but without any artifice or affectation. At a distance he might at first remind you slightly of those pink wax dummies to be seen adopting dandified poses in the window displays of large fashion stores, walking-stick in hand and representing the ideal of male beauty, but closer inspection dispelled any impression of foppishness, for—most unusually—his charm was natural and innate, and seemed an inseparable part of him. He greeted everyone individually in passing, in a manner as warm as it was modest, and it was a pleasure to see his unfailingly graceful demeanour unaffectedly brought into play on every occasion. When a lady was going to the cloakroom he made haste to fetch her coat, he had a friendly glance or joke for every child, he was both affable and discreet—in short, he seemed to be one of those happy souls who, secure in the knowledge that their bright faces and youthful attractions are pleasing to others, transmute that security anew into yet more charm. His presence worked wonders among the hotel guests, most of whom were elderly and sickly, and he irresistibly won everyone's liking with the victorious bearing of youth, that flush of ease and liveliness with which charm so delightfully endows some human beings. Only a couple of hours after his arrival he was playing tennis with the two daughters of the stout, thick-set manufacturer from Lyon—twelve-year-old Annette and thirteen-year-old Blanche—and their mother, the refined, delicate and reserved Madame Henriette, smiled slightly to see her inexperienced daughters unconsciously flirting with the young stranger. That evening he watched for an hour as we played chess, telling a few amusing anecdotes now and then in an unobtrusive style, strolled along the terrace again with Madame Henriette while her husband played dominoes with a business friend as usual; and late in the evening I saw him in suspiciously intimate conversation with the hotel secretary in the dim light of her office. Next morning he went fishing with my Danish chess partner, showing a remarkable knowledge of angling, and then held a long conversation about politics with the Lyon manufacturer in which he also proved himself an entertaining companion, for the stout Frenchman's hearty laughter could be heard above the sound of the breaking waves. After lunch he spent an hour alone with Madame Henriette in the garden again, drinking black coffee, played another game of tennis with her daughters and chatted in the lobby to the German couple. At six o'clock I met him at the railway station when I went to post a letter. He strode quickly towards me and said, as if apologetically, that he had been suddenly called away but would be back in two days' time. Sure enough, he was absent from the dining room that evening, but only in person, for he was the sole subject of conversation at every table, and all the guests praised his delightful, cheerful nature.

That night, I suppose at about eleven o'clock, I was sitting in my room finishing a book when I suddenly heard agitated shouts and cries from the garden coming in through my open window. Something was obviously going on over at the hotel. Feeling concerned rather than curious, I immediately hurried across—it was some fifty paces—and found the guests and staff milling around in great excitement. Madame Henriette, whose husband had been playing dominoes with his friend from Namur as usual, had not come back from her evening walk on the terrace by the beach, and it was feared that she had suffered an accident. The normally ponderous, slow-moving manufacturer kept charging down to the beach like a bull, and when he called: "Henriette! Henriette!" into the night, his voice breaking with fear, the sound conveyed something of the terror and the primeval nature of a gigantic animal wounded to death. The waiters and pageboys ran up and down the stairs in agitation, all the guests were woken and the police were called. The fat man, however, trampled and stumbled his way through all this, waistcoat unbuttoned, sobbing and shrieking as he pointlessly shouted the name "Henriette! Henriette!" into the darkness. By now the children were awake upstairs, and stood at the window in their night dresses, calling down for their mother. Their father hurried upstairs again to comfort them.

And then something so terrible happened that it almost defies retelling, for a violent strain on human nature, at moments of extremity, can often give such tragic expression to a man's bearing that no images or words can reproduce it with the same lightning force. Suddenly the big, heavy man came down the creaking stairs with a changed look on his face, very weary and yet grim. He had a letter in his hand. "Call them all back!" he told the hotel major-domo, in a barely audible voice. "Call everyone in again. There's no need. My wife has left me."

Mortally wounded as he was, the man showed composure, a tense, superhuman composure as he faced all the people standing around, looking at him curiously as they pressed close and then suddenly turned away again, each of them feeling alarmed, ashamed and confused. He had just enough strength left to make his way unsteadily past us, looking at no one, and switch off the light in the reading room. We heard the sound of his ponderous, massive body dropping heavily into an armchair, and then a wild, animal sobbing, the weeping of a man who has never wept before. That elemental pain had a kind of paralysing power over every one of us, even the least of those present. None of the waiters, none of the guests who had joined the throng out of curiosity, ventured either a smile or a word of condolence. Silently, one by one, as if put to shame by so shattering an emotional outburst, we crept back to our rooms, while that stricken specimen of mankind shook and sobbed alone with himself in the dark as the building slowly laid itself to rest, whispering, muttering, murmuring and sighing.

You will understand that such an event, striking like lightning before our very eyes and our perceptions, was likely to cause considerable turmoil in persons usually accustomed to an easygoing existence and carefree pastimes. But while this extraordinary incident was certainly the point of departure for the discussion that broke out so vehemently at our table, almost bringing us to blows, in essence the dispute was more fundamental, an angry conflict between two warring concepts of life. For it soon became known from the indiscretion of a chambermaid who had read the letter—in his helpless fury, the devastated husband had crumpled it up and dropped it on the floor somewhere—that Madame Henriette had not left alone but, by mutual agreement, with the young Frenchman (for whom most people's liking now swiftly began to evaporate). At first glance, of course, it might seem perfectly understandable for this minor Madame Bovary to exchange her stout, provincial husband for an elegant and handsome young fellow. But what aroused so much indignation in all present was the circumstance that neither the manufacturer nor his daughters, nor even Madame Henriette herself, had ever set eyes on this Lovelace before, and consequently their evening conversation for a couple of hours on the terrace, and the one-hour session in the garden over black coffee, seemed to have sufficed to make a woman about thirty-three years old and of blameless reputation abandon her husband and two children overnight, following a young dandy previously unknown to her without a second thought. This apparently evident fact was unanimously condemned at our table as perfidious deceit and a cunning manoeuvre on the part of the two lovers: of course Madame Henriette must have been conducting a clandestine affair with the young man long before, and he had come here, Pied Piper that he was, only to settle the final details of their flight, for—so our company deduced—it was out of the question for a decent woman who had known a man a mere couple of hours to run off just like that when he first whistled her up. It amused me to take a different view, and I energetically defended such an eventuality as possible, even probable in a woman who at heart had perhaps been ready to take some decisive action through all the years of a tedious, disappointing marriage. My unexpected opposition quickly made the discussion more general, and it became particularly agitated when both married couples, the Germans and the Italians alike, denied the existence of the *coup de foudre* with positively scornful indignation, condemning it as folly and tasteless romantic fantasy.

Well, it's of no importance here to go back in every detail over the stormy course of an argument conducted between soup and dessert: only professionals of the table d'hôte are witty, and points made in the heat of a chance dispute at table are usually banal, since the speakers resort to them clumsily and in haste. It is also difficult to explain how our discussion came to assume the form of insulting remarks so quickly; I think it grew so vehement in the first place because of the instinctive wish of both husbands to reassure themselves that their own wives were incapable of such shallow inconstancy. Unfortunately they could find no better way of expressing their feelings than to tell me that no one could speak as I did except a man who judged the feminine psyche by a bachelor's random conquests, which came only too cheap. This accusation rather annoyed me, and when the German lady added her mite by remarking instructively that there were real women on the one hand and 'natural-born tarts' on the other, and in her opinion Madame Henriette must have been one of the latter, I lost patience entirely and became aggressive myself. Such a denial of the obvious fact that at certain times in her life a woman is delivered up to mysterious powers beyond her own will and judgement, I said, merely concealed fear of our own instincts, of the demonic element in our nature, and many people seemed to take pleasure in feeling themselves stronger, purer and more moral than those who are 'easily led astray'. Personally, I added, I thought it more honourable for a woman to follow her instincts freely and passionately than to betray her husband in his own arms with her eyes closed, as so many did. Such, roughly, was the gist of my remarks, and the more the others attacked poor Madame Henriette in a conversation now rising to fever pitch, the more passionately I defended her (going far beyond what I actually felt in the case). My enthusiasm amounted to what in student circles might have been described as a challenge to the two married couples, and as a not very harmonious quartet they went for me with such indignant solidarity that the old Dane, who was sitting there with a jovial expression, much like the referee at a football match with stopwatch in hand, had to tap his knuckles on the table from time to time in admonishment. "Gentlemen, please!" But it never worked for long. One of the husbands had jumped up from the table three times already, red in the face, and could be calmed by his wife only with difficulty—in short, a dozen minutes more and our discussion would have ended in violence, had not Mrs C suddenly poured oil on the stormy waters of the conversation.

Mrs C, the white-haired, distinguished old English lady, presided over our table as unofficial arbiter. Sitting very upright in her place, turning to everyone with the same uniform friendliness, saying little and yet listening with the most gratifying interest, she was a pleasing sight from the purely physical viewpoint, and an air of wonderfully calm composure emanated from her aristocratically reserved nature. Up to a certain point she kept her distance from the rest of us, although she could also show special kindness with tactful delicacy: she spent most of her time in the garden reading books, and sometimes played the piano, but she was seldom to be seen in company or deep in conversation. You scarcely noticed her, yet she exerted a curious influence over us all, for no sooner did she now, for the first time, intervene in our discussion than we all felt, with embarrassment, that we had been too loud and intemperate.

Mrs C had made use of the awkward pause when the German gentleman jumped brusquely up and was then induced to sit quietly down again. Unexpectedly, she raised her clear, grey eyes, looked at me indecisively for a moment, and then, with almost objective clarity, took up the subject in her own way.

"So you think, if I understand you correctly, that Madame Henriette—that a woman can be cast unwittingly into a sudden adventure, can do things that she herself would have thought impossible an hour earlier, and for which she can hardly be held responsible?"

"I feel sure of it, ma'am."

"But then all moral judgements would be meaningless, and any kind of vicious excess could be justified. If you really think that a *crime passionnel*, as the French call it, is no crime at all, then what is the state judiciary for? It doesn't take a great deal of good will—and you yourself have a remarkable amount of that," she added, with a slight smile, "to see passion in every crime, and use that passion to excuse it."

The clear yet almost humorous tone of her words did me good, and instinctively adopting her objective stance I answered half in jest, half in earnest myself: "I'm sure that the state judiciary takes a more severe view of such things than I do; its duty is to protect morality and convention without regard for pity, so it is obliged to judge and make no excuses. But as a private person I don't see why I should voluntarily assume the role of public prosecutor. I'd prefer to appear for the defence. Personally, I'd rather understand others than condemn them."

Mrs C looked straight at me for a while with her clear grey eyes, and hesitated. I began to fear she had failed to understand what I said, and was preparing to repeat it in English. But with a curious gravity, as if conducting an examination, she continued with her questions.

"Don't you think it contemptible or shocking, though, for a woman to leave her husband and her children to follow some chance-met man, when she can't even know if he is worth her love? Can you really excuse such reckless, promiscuous conduct in a woman who is no longer in her first youth, and should have disciplined herself to preserve her self-respect, if only for the sake of her children?"

"I repeat, ma'am," I persisted, "that I decline to judge or condemn her in this case. To you, I can readily admit that I was exaggerating a little just now—poor Madame Henriette is certainly no heroine, not even an adventuress by nature, let alone a *grande amoureuse*. So far as I know her, she seems to me just an average, fallible woman. I do feel a little respect for her because she bravely followed the dictates of her own will, but even more pity, since tomorrow, if not today, she is sure to be deeply unhappy. She may have acted unwisely and certainly too hastily, but her conduct was not base or mean, and I still challenge anyone's right to despise the poor unfortunate woman."

"And what about you yourself; do you still feel exactly the same respect and esteem for her? Don't you see any difference between the woman you knew the day before yesterday as a respectable wife, and the woman who ran off with a perfect stranger a day later?"

"None at all. Not the slightest, not the least difference."

"*Is that so?*" She instinctively spoke those words in English; the whole conversation seemed to be occupying her mind to a remarkable degree. After a brief moment's thought, she raised her clear eyes to me again, with a question in them.

"And suppose you were to meet Madame Henriette tomorrow, let's say in Nice on the young man's arm, would you still greet her?"

"Of course."

"And speak to her?"

"Of course."

"If… if you were married, would you introduce such a woman to your wife as if nothing had happened?"

"Of course."

"*Would you really?*" she said, in English again, speaking in tones of incredulous astonishment.

"*Indeed I would*," I answered, unconsciously falling into English too.

Mrs C was silent. She still seemed to be thinking hard, and suddenly, looking at me as if amazed at her own courage, she said: "I don't know if I would. Perhaps I might." And with the indefinable and peculiarly English ability to end a conversation firmly but without brusque discourtesy, she rose and offered me her hand in a friendly gesture. Her intervention had restored peace, and we were all privately grateful to her for ensuring that although we had been at daggers drawn a moment ago, we could speak to each other with tolerable civility again. The dangerously charged atmosphere was relieved by a few light remarks.

Although our discussion seemed to have been courteously resolved, its irate bitterness had none the less left a faint, lingering sense of estrangement between me and my opponents in argument. The German couple behaved with reserve, while over the next few days the two Italians enjoyed asking me ironically, at frequent intervals, whether I had heard anything of '*la cara signora Henrietta*'. Urbane as our manners might appear, something of the equable, friendly good fellowship of our table had been irrevocably destroyed.

The chilly sarcasm of my adversaries was made all the more obvious by the particular friendliness Mrs C had shown me since our discussion. Although she was usually very reserved, and hardly ever seemed to invite conversation with her table companions outside meal times, she now on several occasions found an opportunity to speak to me in the garden and—I might almost say—distinguish me by her attention, for her upper-class reserve made a private talk with her seem a special favour. To be honest, in fact, I must say she positively sought me out and took every opportunity of entering into conversation with me, in so marked a way that had she not been a white-haired elderly lady I might have entertained some strange, conceited ideas. But when we talked our conversation inevitably and without fail came back to the same point of departure, to Madame Henriette: it seemed to give her some mysterious pleasure to accuse the errant wife of weakness of character and irresponsibility. At the same time, however, she seemed to enjoy my steadfast defence of that refined and delicate woman, and my insistence that nothing could ever make me deny my sympathy for her. She constantly steered our conversation the same way, and in the end I hardly knew what to make of her strange, almost eccentric obsession with the subject.

This went on for a few days, maybe five or six, and she never said a word to suggest why this kind of conversation had assumed importance for her. But I could not help realising that it had when I happened to mention, during a walk, that my stay here would soon be over, and I thought of leaving the day after tomorrow. At this her usually serene face suddenly assumed a curiously intense expression, and something like the shadow of a cloud came into her clear grey eyes. "Oh, what a pity! There's still so much I'd have liked to discuss with you." And from then on a certain uneasy restlessness showed that while she spoke she was thinking of something else, something that occupied and distracted her mind a great deal. At last she herself seemed disturbed by this mental distraction, for in the middle of a silence that had suddenly fallen between us she unexpectedly offered me her hand.

"I see that I can't put what I really want to say to you clearly. I'd rather write it down." And walking faster than I was used to seeing her move, she went towards the house.

I did indeed find a letter in her energetic, frank handwriting in my room just before dinner that evening. I now greatly regret my carelessness with written documents in my youth, which means that I cannot reproduce her note word for word, and can give only the gist of her request: might she, she asked, tell me about an episode in her life? It lay so far back in the past, she wrote, that it was hardly a part of her present existence any more, and the fact that I was leaving the day after tomorrow made it easier for her to speak of something that had occupied and preyed on her mind for over twenty years. If I did not feel such a conversation was an importunity, she would like to ask me for an hour of my time.

The letter—I merely outline its contents here—fascinated me to an extraordinary degree: its English style alone lent it great clarity and resolution. Yet I did not find it easy to answer. I tore up three drafts before I replied:

> *I am honoured by your showing such confidence in me, and I promise you an honest response should you require one. Of course I cannot ask you to tell me more than your heart dictates. But whatever you tell, tell yourself and me the truth. Please believe me: I feel your confidence a special honour.*

The note made its way to her room that evening, and I received the answer next morning:

> *You are quite right: half the truth is useless, only the whole truth is worth telling. I shall do my best to hide nothing from myself or from you. Please come to my room after dinner—at the age of sixty-seven, I need fear no misinterpretation, but I cannot speak freely in the garden, or with other people near by. Believe me, I did not find it easy to make my mind up to take this step.*

During the day we met again at table and discussed indifferent matters in the conventional way. But when we encountered each other in the garden she avoided me in obvious confusion, and I felt it both painful and moving to see this white-haired old lady fleeing from me down an avenue lined with pine trees, as shy as a young girl.

At the appointed time that evening I knocked on her door, and it was immediately opened; the room was bathed in soft twilight, with only the little reading lamp on the table casting a circle of yellow light in the dusk. Mrs C came towards me without any self-consciousness, offered me an armchair and sat down opposite me. I sensed that she had prepared mentally for each of these movements, but then came a pause, obviously unplanned, a pause that grew longer and longer as she came to a difficult decision. I dared not inject any remark into this pause, for I sensed a strong will wrestling with great resistance here. Sometimes the faint notes of a waltz drifted up from the drawing room below, and I listened intently, as if to relieve the silence of some of its oppressive quality. She too seemed to feel the unnatural tension of the silence awkward, for she suddenly pulled herself together to take the plunge, and began.

"It's only the first few words that are so difficult. For the last two days I have been preparing to be perfectly clear and truthful; I hope I shall succeed. Perhaps you don't yet understand why I am telling all this to you, a stranger, but not a day, scarcely an hour goes by when I do not think of this particular incident, and you can believe me, an old woman now, when I say it is intolerable to spend one's whole life staring at a single point in it, a single day. Everything I am about to tell you, you see, happened within the space of just twenty-four hours in my sixty-seven years of life, and I have often asked myself, I have wondered to the point of madness, why a moment's foolish action on a single occasion should matter. But we cannot shake off what we so vaguely call conscience, and when I heard you speak so objectively of Madame Henriette's case I thought that perhaps there might be an end to my senseless dwelling on the past, my constant self-accusation, if I could bring myself to speak freely to someone, anyone, about that single day in my life. If I were not an Anglican but a Catholic, the confessional would long ago have offered me an opportunity of release by putting what I have kept silent into words—but that comfort is denied us, and so I make this strange attempt to absolve myself by speaking to you today. I know all this sounds very odd, but you agreed unhesitatingly to my suggestion, and I am grateful.

As I said, I would like to tell you about just one day in my life—all the rest of it seems to me insignificant and would be tedious listening for anyone else. There was nothing in the least out of the ordinary in the course of it until my forty-second year. My parents were rich landlords in Scotland, we owned large factories and leased out land, and in the usual way of the gentry in my country we spent most of the year on our estates but went to London for the season. I met my future husband at a party when I was eighteen. He was a second son of the well-known R family, and had served with the army in India for ten years. We soon married, and led the carefree life of our social circle: three months of the year in London, three months on our estates, and the rest of the time in hotels in Italy, Spain and France. Not the slightest shadow ever clouded our marriage, and we had two sons who are now grown up. When I was forty my husband suddenly died. He had returned from his years in the tropics with a liver complaint, and I lost him within the space of two terrible weeks. My elder son was already in the army, my younger son at university—so I was left entirely alone overnight, and used as I was to affectionate companionship, that loneliness was a torment to me. I felt I could not stay a day longer in the desolate house where every object reminded me of the tragic loss of my beloved husband, and so I decided that while my sons were still unmarried, I would spend much of the next few years travelling.

In essence, I regarded my life from that moment on as entirely pointless and useless. The man with whom I had shared every hour and every thought for twenty-three years was dead, my children did not need me, I was afraid of casting a cloud over their youth with my sadness and melancholy—but I wished and desired nothing any more for myself. I went first to Paris, where I visited shops and museums out of sheer boredom, but the city and everything else were strange to me, and I avoided company because I could not bear the polite sympathy in other people's eyes when they saw that I was in mourning. How those months of aimless, apathetic wandering passed I can hardly say now; all I know is that I had a constant wish to die, but not the strength to hasten the end I longed for so ardently.

In my second year of mourning, that is to say my forty-second year, I had come to Monte Carlo at the end of March in my unacknowledged flight from time that had become worthless and was more than I could deal with. To be honest, I came there out of tedium, out of the painful emptiness of the heart that wells up like nausea, and at least tries to nourish itself on small external stimulations. The less I felt in myself, the more strongly I was drawn to those places where the whirligig of life spins most rapidly. If you are experiencing nothing yourself, the passionate restlessness of others stimulates the nervous system like music or drama.

That was why I quite often went to the casino. I was intrigued to see the tide of delight or dismay ebbing and flowing in other people's faces, while my own heart lay at such a low ebb. In addition my husband, although never frivolous, had enjoyed visiting such places now and then, and with a certain unintentional piety I remained faithful to his old habits. And there in the casino began those twenty-four hours that were more thrilling than any game, and disturbed my life for years.

I had dined at midday with the Duchess of M, a relation of my family, and after supper I didn't feel tired enough to go to bed yet. So I went to the gaming hall, strolled among the tables without playing myself, and watched the mingled company in my own special way. I repeat, in my own special way, the way my dead husband had once taught me when, tired of watching, I complained of the tedium of looking at the same faces all the time: the wizened old women who sat for hours before venturing a single jetton, the cunning professionals, the *demi-mondaines* of the card table, all that dubious chance-met company which, as you'll know, is considerably less picturesque and romantic than it is always painted in silly novels, where you might think it the *fleur d'élégance* and aristocracy of Europe. Yet the casino of twenty years ago, when real money, visible and tangible, was staked and crackling banknotes, gold Napoleons and pert little five-franc pieces rained down, was far more attractive than it is today, with a solid set of folk on Cook's Tours tediously frittering their characterless gaming chips away in the grand, fashionably renovated citadel of gambling. Even then, however, I found little to stimulate me in the similarity of so many indifferent faces, until one day my husband, whose private passion was for chiromancy—that's to say, divination by means of the hand—showed me an unusual method of observation which proved much more interesting, exciting and fascinating than standing casually around. In this method you never look at a face, only at the rectangle of the table, and on the table only at the hands of the players and the way they move. I don't know if you yourself ever happen to have looked at the green table, just that green square with the ball in the middle of it tumbling drunkenly from number to number, while fluttering scraps of paper, round silver and gold coins fall like seedcorn on the spaces of the board, to be raked briskly away by the croupier or shovelled over to the winner like harvest bounty. If you watch from that angle, only the hands change—all those pale, moving, waiting hands around the green table, all emerging from the ever-different caverns of the players' sleeves, each a beast of prey ready to leap, each varying in shape and colour, some bare, others laden with rings and clinking bracelets, some hairy like wild beasts, some damp and writhing like eels, but all of them tense, vibrating with a vast impatience. I could never help thinking of a racecourse where the excited horses are held back with difficulty on the starting line in case they gallop away too soon; they quiver and buck and rear in just the same way. You can tell everything from those hands, from the way they wait, they grab, they falter; you can see an avaricious character in a claw-like hand and a spendthrift in a relaxed one, a calculating man in a steady hand and a desperate man in a trembling wrist; hundreds of characters betray themselves instantly in their way of handling money, crumpling or nervously creasing notes, or letting it lie as the ball goes round, their hands now weary and exhausted. Human beings give themselves away in play—a cliché, I know, but I would say their own hands give them away even more clearly in gambling. Almost all gamblers soon learn to control their faces—from the neck up, they wear the cold mask of impassivity; they force away the lines around their mouths and hide their agitation behind clenched teeth, they refuse to let their eyes show uneasiness, they smooth the twitching muscles of the face into an artificial indifference, obeying the dictates of polite conduct. But just because their whole attention is concentrated on controlling the face, the most visible part of the body, they forget their hands, they forget that some people are watching nothing but those hands, guessing from them what the lips curved in a smile, the intentionally indifferent glances wish to conceal. Meanwhile, however, their hands shamelessly reveal their innermost secrets. For a moment inevitably comes when all those carefully controlled, apparently relaxed fingers drop their elegant negligence. In the pregnant moment when the roulette ball drops into its shallow compartment and the winning number is called, in that second every one of those hundred or five hundred hands spontaneously makes a very personal, very individual movement of primitive instinct. And if an observer like me, particularly well-informed as I was because of my husband's hobby, is used to watching the hands perform in this arena, it is more exciting even than music or drama to see so many different temperaments suddenly erupt.

I simply cannot tell you how many thousands of varieties of hands there are: wild beasts with hairy, crooked fingers raking in the money like spiders; nervous, trembling hands with pale nails that scarcely dare to touch it; hands noble and vulgar, hands brutal and shy, cunning hands, hands that seem to be stammering—but each of these pairs of hands is different, the expression of an individual life, with the exception of the four or five pairs of hands belonging to the croupiers. Those hands are entirely mechanical, and with their objective, businesslike, totally detached precision function like the clicking metal mechanism of a gas meter by comparison with the extreme liveliness of the gamblers' hands. But even those sober hands produce a surprising effect when contrasted with their racing, passionate fellows; you might say they were wearing a different uniform, like policemen in the middle of a surging, agitated riot. And then there is the personal incentive of getting to know the many different habits and passions of individual pairs of hands within a few days; by then I had always made acquaintances among them and divided them, as if they were human beings, into those I liked and those I did not. I found the greed and incivility of some so repulsive that I would always avert my gaze from them, as if from some impropriety. Every new pair of hands to appear on the table, however, was a fresh experience and a source of curiosity to me; I often quite forgot to look at the face which, surrounded by a collar high above them, was set impassively on top of an evening shirt or a glittering décolletage, a cold social mask.

When I entered the gaming hall that evening, passed two crowded tables, reached a third, and was taking out a few coins,

I was surprised to hear a very strange sound directly opposite me in the wordless, tense pause that seems to echo with silence and always sets in as the ball, moving sluggishly, hesitates between two numbers. It was a cracking, clicking sound like the snapping of joints. I looked across the table in amazement. And then I saw—I was truly startled!—I saw two hands such as I had never seen before, left and right clutching each other like doggedly determined animals, bracing and extending together and against one another with such heightened tension that the fingers' joints cracked with a dry sound like a nut cracking open. They were hands of rare beauty, unusually long, unusually slender, yet taut and muscular—very white, the nails pale at their tips, gently curving and the colour of mother-of-pearl. I kept watching them all evening, indeed I kept marvelling at those extraordinary, those positively unique hands—but what surprised and alarmed me so much at first was the passion in them, their crazily impassioned expressiveness, the convulsive way they wrestled with and supported each other. I knew at once that I was seeing a human being overflowing with emotion, forcing his passion into his fingertips lest it tear him apart. And then—just as the ball, with a dry click, fell into place in the wheel and the croupier called out the number—at that very moment the two hands suddenly fell apart like a pair of animals struck by a single bullet. They dropped, both of them, truly dead and not just exhausted; they dropped with so graphic an expression of lethargy, disappointment, instant extinction, as if all was finally over, that I can find no words to describe it. For never before or since have I seen such speaking hands, hands in which every muscle was eloquent and passion broke almost tangibly from the pores of the skin. They lay on the green table for a moment like jellyfish cast up by the sea, flat and dead. Then one of them, the right hand, began laboriously raising itself again, beginning with the fingertips; it quivered, drew back, turned on itself, swayed, circled, and suddenly reached nervously for a jetton, rolling the token uncertainly like a little wheel between the tips of thumb and middle finger. And suddenly it arched, like a panther arching its back, and shot forwards, positively spitting the hundred-franc jetton out on the middle of the black space. At once, as if at a signal, the inactive, slumbering left hand was seized by excitement too; it rose, slunk, crawled over to its companion hand, which was trembling now as if exhausted by throwing down the jetton, and both hands lay there together trembling, the joints of their fingers working away soundlessly on the table, tapping slightly together like teeth chattering in a fever—no, I had never seen hands of such expressive eloquence, or such spasmodic agitation and tension. Everything else in this vaulted room, the hum from the other halls around it, the calls of the croupiers crying their wares like market traders, the movement of people and of the ball itself which now, dropped from above, was leaping like a thing possessed around the circular cage that was smooth as parquet flooring—all this diversity of whirling, swirling impressions flitting across the nerves suddenly seemed to me dead and dull compared to those two trembling, breathing, gasping, waiting, freezing hands, that extraordinary pair of hands which somehow held me spellbound.

But finally I could no longer refrain; I had to see the human being, the face to which those magical hands belonged, and fearfully—yes, I do mean fearfully, for I was afraid of those hands!—my gaze slowly travelled up the gambler's sleeves and narrow shoulders. And once again I had a shock, for his face spoke the same fantastically extravagant language of extremes as the hands, shared the same terrible grimness of expression and delicate, almost feminine beauty. I had never seen such a face before, a face so transported and utterly beside itself, and I had plenty of opportunity to observe it at leisure as if it were a mask, an unseeing sculpture: those possessed eyes did not turn to right or left for so much as a second, their pupils were fixed and black beneath the widely opened lids, dead glass balls reflecting that other mahogany-coloured ball rolling and leaping about the roulette wheel in such foolish high spirits. Never, I repeat, had I seen so intense or so fascinating a face. It belonged to a young man of perhaps twenty-four, it was fine-drawn, delicate, rather long and very expressive. Like the hands, it did not seem entirely masculine, but resembled the face of a boy passionately absorbed in a game—although I noticed none of that until later, for now the face was entirely veiled by an expression of greed and of madness breaking out. The thin mouth, thirsting and open, partly revealed the teeth: you could see them ten paces away, grinding feverishly while the parted lips remained rigid. A light-blond lock of hair clung damply to his forehead, tumbling forwards like the hair of a man falling, and a tic fluttered constantly around his nostrils as if little waves were invisibly rippling beneath the skin. The bowed head was moving instinctively further and further forwards; you felt it was being swept away with the whirling of the little ball, and now, for the first time, I understood the convulsive pressure of the hands. Only by the intense strain of pressing them together did the body, falling from its central axis, contrive to keep its balance. I had never—I must repeat it yet again—I had never seen a face in which passion showed so openly, with such shamelessly naked animal feeling, and I stared at that face, as fascinated and spellbound by its obsession as was its own gaze by the leaping, twitching movement of the circling ball. From that moment on I noticed nothing else in the room, everything seemed to me dull, dim and blurred, dark by comparison with the flashing fire of that face, and disregarding everyone else present I spent perhaps an hour watching that one man and every movement he made: the bright light that sparkled in his eyes, the convulsive knot of his hands loosening as if blown apart by an explosion, the parting of the shaking fingers as the croupier pushed twenty gold coins towards their eager grasp. At that moment the face looked suddenly bright and very young, the lines in it smoothed out, the eyes began to gleam, the convulsively bowed body straightened lightly, easily—he suddenly sat there as relaxed as a horseman, borne up by the sense of triumph, fingers toying lovingly, idly with the round coins, clinking them together, making them dance and jingle playfully. Then he turned his head restlessly again, surveyed the green table as if with the flaring nostrils of a young hound seeking the right scent, and suddenly, with one quick movement, placed all the coins on one rectangular space. At once the watchfulness, the tension returned. Once more the little waves, rippling galvanically, spread out from his lips, once again his hands were clasped, the boyish face disappeared behind greedy expectation until the spasmodic tension exploded and fell apart in disappointment: the face that had just looked boyish turned faded, wan and old, light disappeared from the burnt-out eyes, and all this within the space of a second as the ball came to rest on the wrong number. He had lost; he stared at the ball for a few seconds almost like an idiot, as if he did not understand, but as the croupier began calling to whip up interest, his fingers took out a few coins again. But his certainty was gone; first he put the coins on one space, then, thinking better of it, on another, and when the ball had begun to roll his trembling hand, on a sudden impulse, quickly added two crumpled banknotes.

This alternation of up and down, loss and gain, continued without a break for about an hour, and during that hour I did not, even for a moment, take my fascinated gaze from that ever-changing face and all the passions ebbing and flowing over it. I kept my eyes fixed on those magical hands, their every muscle graphically reflecting the whole range of the man's feelings as they rose and fell like a fountain. I had never watched the face of an actor in the theatre as intently as I watched this one, seeing the constant, changing shades of emotion flitting over it like light and shade moving over a landscape. I had never immersed myself so wholeheartedly in a game as I did in the reflection of this stranger's excitement. If someone had been observing me at that moment he would surely have taken my steely gaze for a state of hypnosis, and indeed my benumbed perception was something like that—I simply could not look away from the play of those features, and everything else in the room, the lights, the laughter, the company and its glances, merely drifted vaguely around me, a yellow mist with that face in the middle of it, a flame among flames. I heard nothing, I felt nothing, I did not notice people coming forwards beside me, other hands suddenly reaching out like feelers, putting down money or picking it up; I did not see the ball or hear the croupier's voice, yet I saw it all as if I were dreaming, exaggerated as in a concave mirror by the excitement and extravagance of those moving hands. For I did not have to look at the roulette wheel to know whether the ball had come to rest on red or black, whether it was still rolling or beginning to falter. Every stage of the game, loss and gain, hope and disappointment, was fierily reflected in the nerves and movements of that passionate face.

But then came a terrible moment—something that I had been vaguely fearing all this time, something that had weighed like a gathering thunderstorm on my tense nerves, and now suddenly ripped through them. Yet again the ball had fallen back into the shallow depression with that dry little click, yet again came the tense moment when two hundred lips held their breath until the croupier's voice announced the winning number—this time it was zero—while he zealously raked in the clinking coins and crackling notes from all sides. At that moment those two convulsively clasped hands made a particularly terrifying movement, leaping up as if to catch something that wasn't there and then dropping to the table again exhausted, with no strength in them, only the force of gravity flooding back. Then, however, they suddenly came to life yet again, feverishly retreating from the table to the man's own body, clambering up his torso like wild cats, up and down, left and right, nervously trying all his pockets to see if some forgotten coin might not have slipped into one of them. But they always came back empty, and the pointless, useless search began again ever more frantically, while the roulette wheel went on circling and others continued playing, while coins clinked, chairs were shifted on the floor, and all the small sounds, put together a hundredfold, filled the room with a humming note. I trembled, shaking with horror; I felt it all as clearly as if my own fingers were rummaging desperately for a coin in the pockets and folds of my creased garments. And suddenly, with a single abrupt movement, the man rose to his feet opposite me, like a man standing up when he suddenly feels unwell and must rise if he is not to suffocate. His chair crashed to the floor behind him. Without even noticing, without paying any attention to his surprised and abashed neighbours as they avoided his swaying figure, he stumbled away from the table.

The sight petrified me. For I knew at once where the man was going: to his death. A man getting to his feet like that was not on his way back to an inn, a wine bar, a wife, a railway carriage, to any form of life at all, he was plunging straight into the abyss. Even the most hardened spectator in that hellish gaming hall could surely have seen that the man had nothing to fall back on, not at home or in a bank or with a family, but had been sitting here with the last of his money, staking his life, and was now staggering away somewhere else, anywhere, but undoubtedly out of that life. I had feared all along, I had sensed from the first moment, as if by magic, that more than loss or gain was staked on the game, yet now it struck me like a bolt of dark lightning to see the life suddenly go out of his eyes and death cast its pale shadow over his still living face. Instinctively—affected as I was by his own graphic gestures—I clutched at myself while the man tore himself away from his place and staggered out, for his own uncertain gait was now transferred to my own body just as his tension had entered my veins and nerves. Then I was positively wrenched away, I had to follow him; my feet moved without my own volition. It was entirely unconscious, I did not do it of my own accord, it was something happening to me when, taking no notice of anyone, feeling nothing myself, I went out into the corridor leading to the doors.

He was standing at the cloakroom counter, and the attendant had brought him his coat. But his arms would no longer obey him, so the helpful attendant laboriously eased them into the sleeves, as if he were paralysed. I saw him automatically put his hand in his waistcoat pocket to give the man a tip, but his fingers emerged empty. Then he suddenly seemed to remember everything, awkwardly stammered something to the cloakroom attendant, and as before moved forwards abruptly and then stumbled like a drunk down the casino steps, where the attendant stood briefly watching him go, with a smile that was at first contemptuous and then understanding.

His bearing shook me so much that I felt ashamed to have seen it. Involuntarily I turned aside, embarrassed to have watched a stranger's despair as if I were in a theatre—but then that vague fear suddenly took me out of myself once again. Quickly, I retrieved my coat, and thinking nothing very definite, purely mechanically and compulsively I hurried out into the dark after the stranger."

*

Mrs C interrupted her story for a moment. She had been sitting calmly opposite me, speaking almost without a break with her characteristic tranquil objectivity, as only someone who had prepared and carefully organised the events of her tale in advance could speak. Now, for the first time, she stopped, hesitated, and then suddenly broke off and turned directly to me.

"I promised you and myself," she began, rather unevenly, "to tell you all the facts with perfect honesty. Now I must ask you to believe in my honesty, and not assume that my conduct had any ulterior motives. I might not be ashamed of them today, but in this case such suspicions would be entirely unfounded. And I must emphasise that, when I hurried after that ruined gambler in the street, I had certainly not fallen in love with him—I did not think of him as a man at all, and indeed I was over forty myself at the time and had never looked at another man since my husband's death. All that part of my life was finally over; I tell you this explicitly, and I must, or you would not understand the full horror of what happened later. On the other hand, it's true that I would find it difficult to give a clear name to the feeling that drew me so compulsively after the unfortunate man; there was curiosity in it, but above all a dreadful fear, or rather a fear of something dreadful, something I had felt invisibly enveloping the young man like a miasma from the first moment. But such feelings can't be dissected and taken apart, if only because they come over one too compulsively, too fast, too spontaneously—very likely mine expressed nothing but the instinct to help with which one snatches back a child about to run into the road in front of a motor car. How else can we explain why non-swimmers will jump off a bridge to help a drowning man? They are simply impelled to do it as if by magic, some other will pushes them off the bridge before they have time to consider the pointless bravery of their conduct properly; and in just the same way, without thinking, without conscious reflection, I hurried after the unfortunate young man out of the gaming room, to the casino doors, out of the doors and on to the terrace.

And I am sure that neither you nor any other feeling human being with his eyes open could have withstood that fearful curiosity, for a more disturbing sight can hardly be imagined than the way the gambler, who must have been twenty-four at the most but moved as laboriously as an old man and was swaying like a drunk, dragged himself shakily and disjointedly down the steps to the terrace beside the road. Once there, his body dropped on to a bench, limp as a sack. Again I shuddered as I sensed, from that movement, that the man had reached the end of his tether. Only a dead man or one with nothing left to keep him alive drops like that. His head, fallen to one side, leant back over the bench, his arms hung limp and shape-less to the ground, and in the dim illumination of the faintly flickering street lights any passer-by would have thought he had been shot. And it was like that—I can't explain why the vision suddenly came into my mind, but all of a sudden it was there, real enough to touch, terrifying and terrible—it was like that, as a man who had been shot, that I saw him before me at that moment, and I knew for certain that he had a revolver in his pocket, and tomorrow he would be found lying lifeless and covered with blood on this or some other bench. For he had dropped like a stone falling into a deep chasm, never to stop until it reaches the bottom: I never saw such a physical expression of exhaustion and despair.

So now, consider my situation: I was standing twenty or thirty paces from the bench and the motionless, broken man on it, with no idea what to do, on the one hand wishing to help, on the other restrained by my innate and inbred reluctance to speak to a strange man in the street. The gaslights flickered dimly in the overcast sky, few figures hurried past, for it was nearly midnight and I was almost entirely alone in the park with this suicidal figure. Five or ten times I had already pulled myself together and approached him, but shame or perhaps that deeper premonitory instinct, the idea that falling men are likely to pull those who come to their aid down with them, made me withdraw—and in the midst of this indecision I was clearly aware of the pointless, ridiculous aspect of the situation. Nonetheless, I could neither speak nor turn away, I could not do anything but I could not leave him. And I hope you will believe me when I say that for perhaps an hour, an endless hour, I walked indecisively up and down that terrace, while time was divided up by thousands of little sounds from the breaking waves of the invisible sea—so shaken and transfixed was I by the idea of the annihilation of a human being.

Yet I could not summon up the courage to say a word or make a move, and I would have waited like that half the night, or perhaps in the end my wiser self-interest would have prevailed on me to go home, and indeed I think I had already made up my mind to leave that helpless bundle of misery lying there—when a superior force put an end to my indecision. It began to rain. All evening the wind had been piling up heavy spring clouds full of moisture above the sea, lungs and heart felt the pressure of the lowering sky, and now drops suddenly began to splash down. Soon a heavy rain was falling in wet torrents blown about by the wind. I instinctively sheltered under the projecting roof of a kiosk, but although I put up my umbrella gusts of wind kept blowing the rain on my dress. I felt the cold mist thrown up by the falling raindrops spray my face and hands.

But—and it was such a terrible sight that even now, two decades later, the memory still constricts my throat—but in the middle of this cloudburst the unfortunate man stayed perfectly still on his bench, never moving. Water was gurgling and dripping from all the eaves; you could hear the rumble of carriages from the city; people with their coat collars turned up hurried past to right and to left; all living creatures ducked in alarm, fled, ran, sought shelter; man and beast felt universal fear of the torrential element—but that black heap of humanity on the bench did not stir or move. I told you before that he had the magical gift of graphically expressing everything he felt in movement and gesture. But nothing, nothing on earth could convey despair, total self-surrender, death in the midst of life to such shattering effect as his immobility, the way he sat there in the falling rain, not moving, feeling nothing, too tired to rise and walk the few steps to the shelter of the projecting roof, utterly indifferent to his own existence. No sculptor, no poet, not Michelangelo or Dante has ever brought that sense of ultimate despair, of ultimate human misery so feelingly to my mind as the sight of that living figure letting the watery element drench him, too weary and uncaring to make a single move to protect himself.

That made me act; I couldn't help it. Pulling myself together, I ran the gauntlet of the lashing rain and shook the dripping bundle of humanity to make him get up from the bench. 'Come along!' I seized his arm. Something stared up at me, with difficulty. Something in him seemed to be slowly preparing to move, but he did not understand. 'Come along!' Once again, almost angry now, I tugged at his wet sleeve. Then he slowly stood up, devoid of will and swaying. 'What do you want?' he asked, and I could not reply, for I myself had no idea where to take him—just away from the cold downpour where he had been sitting so senselessly, suicidally, in the grip of deep despair. I did not let go of his arm but dragged the man on, since he had no will of his own, to the sales kiosk where the narrow, projecting roof at least partly sheltered him from the raging attack of the stormy rain as the wind tossed it wildly back and forth. That was all I wanted, I had nothing else in mind, just to get him somewhere dry, under a roof. As yet I had thought no further.

So we stood side by side on that narrow strip of dry ground, the wall of the kiosk behind us and above us only the roof, which was not large enough, for the insatiable rain insidiously came in under it as sudden gusts of wind flung wet, chilly showers over our clothes and into our faces. The situation became intolerable. I could hardly stand there any longer beside this dripping wet stranger. On the other hand, having dragged him over here I couldn't just leave him and walk away without a word. Something had to be done, and gradually I forced myself to think clearly. It would be best, I thought, to send him home in a cab and then go home myself; he would be able to look after himself tomorrow. So as he stood beside me gazing fixedly out at the turbulent night I asked, 'Where do you live?'

'I'm not staying anywhere... I only arrived from Nice this morning... we can't go to my place.'

I did not immediately understand this last remark. Only later did I realise that the man took me for... for a *demi-mondaine*, one of the many women who haunt the casino by night, hoping to extract a little money from lucky gamblers or drunks. After all, what else was he to think, for only now that I tell you about it do I feel all the improbability, indeed the fantastic nature of my situation—what else was he to think of me? The way I had pulled him off the bench and dragged him away as if it were perfectly natural was certainly not the conduct of a lady. But this idea did not occur to me at once. Only later, only too late did his terrible misapprehension dawn upon me, or I would never have said what I did next, in words that were bound to reinforce his impression. 'Then we'll just take a room in a hotel. You can't stay here. You must get under cover somewhere.'

Now I understood his painful misunderstanding, for he did not turn towards me but merely rejected the idea with a certain contempt in his voice: 'I don't need a room; I don't need anything now. Don't bother, you won't get anything out of me. You've picked the wrong man. I have no money.'

This too was said in a dreadful tone, with shattering indifference, and the way he stood there dripping wet and leaning against the wall, slack and exhausted to the bone, shook me so much that I had no time to waste on taking petty offence. I merely sensed, as I had from the first moment when I saw him stagger from the gaming hall, as I had felt all through this improbable hour, that here was a human being, a young, living, breathing human being on the very brink of death, and I must save him. I came closer.

'Never mind money, come along! You can't stay here. I'll get you under cover. Don't worry about anything, just come with me.'

He turned his head and I felt, while the rain drummed round us with a hollow sound and the eaves cast water down to splash at our feet, that for the first time he was trying to make out my face in the dark. His body seemed to be slowly shaking off its lethargy too.

'As you like,' he said, giving in. 'It's all one to me… after all, why not? Let's go.' I put up my umbrella, he moved to my side and took my arm. I felt this sudden intimacy uncomfortable; indeed, it horrified me. I was alarmed to the depths of my heart. But I did not feel bold enough to ask him to refrain, for if I rejected him now he would fall into the bottomless abyss, and everything I had tried to do so far would be in vain. We walked the few steps back to the casino, and only now did it strike me that I had no idea what to do with him. I had better take him to a hotel, I thought quickly, and give him money to spend the night there and go home in the morning. I was not thinking beyond that. And as the carriages were now rapidly drawing up outside the casino I hailed a cab and we got in. When the driver asked where to, I couldn't think what to say at first. But realising that the drenched, dripping man beside me would not be welcome in any of the best hotels—on the other hand, genuinely inexperienced as I was, with nothing else in mind—I just told the cabby, 'Some simple hotel, anywhere!'

The driver, indifferent, and wet with rain himself, drove his horses on. The stranger beside me said not a word, the wheels rattled, the rain splashed heavily against the windows, and I felt as if I were travelling with a corpse in that dark, lightless rectangular space, in a vehicle like a coffin. I tried to think of something to say to relieve the strange, silent horror of our presence there together, but I could think of nothing. After a few minutes the cab stopped. I got out first and paid the driver, who shut the door after us as if drunk with sleep. We were at the door of a small hotel that was unknown to me, with a glass porch above us providing a tiny area of shelter from the rain, which was still lashing the impenetrable night around us with ghastly monotony.

The stranger, giving way to his inertia, had instinctively leant against the wall, and water was dripping from his wet hat and crumpled garments. He stood there like a drunk who has been fished out of the river, still dazed, and a channel of water trickling down from him formed around the small patch of ground where he stood. But he made not the slightest effort to shake himself or take off the hat from which raindrops kept running over his forehead and face. He stood there entirely apathetically, and I cannot tell you how his broken demeanour moved me.

But something had to be done. I put my hand into my bag. 'Here are a hundred francs,' I said. 'Take a room and go back to Nice tomorrow.'

He looked up in astonishment.

'I was watching you in the gaming hall,' I continued urgently, noticing his hesitation. 'I know you've lost everything, and I fear you're well on the way to doing something stupid. There's no shame in accepting help—here, take it!'

But he pushed away my hand with an energy I wouldn't have expected in him. 'You are very good,' he said, 'but don't waste your money. There's no help for me now. Whether I sleep tonight or not makes not the slightest difference. It will all be over tomorrow anyway. There's no help for me.'

'No, you must take it,' I urged. 'You'll see things differently tomorrow. Go upstairs and sleep on it. Everything will look different in daylight.'

But when I tried to press the money on him again he pushed my hand away almost violently. 'Don't,' he repeated dully. 'There's no point in it. Better to do it out of doors than leave blood all over their room here. A hundred or even a thousand francs won't help me. I'd just go to the gaming hall again tomorrow with the last few francs, and I wouldn't stop until they were all gone. Why begin again? I've had enough.'

You have no idea how that dull tone of voice went to my heart, but think of it: a couple of inches from you stands a young, bright, living, breathing human being, and you know that if you don't do your utmost, then in a few hours time this thinking, speaking, breathing specimen of youth will be a corpse. And now I felt a desire like rage, like fury, to overcome his senseless resistance. I grasped his arm. 'That's enough stupid talk. You go up these steps now and take a room, and

I'll come in the morning and take you to the station. You must get away from here, you must go home tomorrow, and I won't rest until I've seen you sitting in the train with a ticket. You can't throw your life away so young just because you've lost a couple of hundred francs, or a couple of thousand. That's cowardice, silly hysteria concocted from anger and bitterness. You'll see that I'm right tomorrow!'

'Tomorrow!' he repeated in a curiously gloomy, ironic tone. 'Tomorrow! If you knew where I'd be tomorrow! I wish I knew myself—I'm mildly curious to find out. No, go home, my dear, don't bother about me and don't waste your money.'

But I wasn't giving up now. It had become like a mania obsessing me. I took his hand by force and pressed the banknote into it. 'You will take this money and go in at once!' And so saying I stepped firmly up to the door and rang the bell. 'There, now I've rung, and the porter will be here in a minute. Go in and lie down. I'll be outside here at nine tomorrow to take you straight to the station. Don't worry about anything, I'll see to what's necessary to get you home. But now go to bed, have a good sleep, and don't think of anything else!'

At that moment the key turned inside the door and the porter opened it.

'Come on, then!' said my companion suddenly, in a harsh, firm embittered voice, and I felt his fingers span my wrist in an iron grip. I was alarmed… so greatly alarmed, so paralysed, struck as if by lightning, that all my composure vanished. I wanted to resist, tear myself away, but my will seemed numbed, and I… well, you will understand… I was ashamed to struggle with a stranger in front of the porter, who stood there waiting impatiently. And so, suddenly, I was inside the hotel. I wanted to speak, say something, but my throat would not obey me… and his hand lay heavy and commanding on my arm. I vaguely felt it draw me as if unawares up a flight of steps—a key clicked in a lock. And suddenly I was alone with this stranger in a strange room, in some hotel whose name I do not know to this day."

Mrs C stopped again, and suddenly rose to her feet. It seemed that her voice would not obey her any more. She went over to the window and looked out in silence for some minutes, or perhaps she was just resting her forehead on the cold pane; I did not have the courage to look closely, for I found it painful to see the old lady so agitated. So I sat quite still, asking no questions, making no sound, and waited until she came back, stepping firmly, and sat down opposite me.

"Well—now the most difficult part is told. And I hope you will believe me when I assure you yet again, when I swear by all that is sacred to me, by my honour and my children, that up to that moment no idea of any… any relationship with the stranger had entered my mind, that I really had been suddenly plunged into this situation against my own will, indeed entirely unawares, as if I had fallen through a trapdoor from the level path of my existence. I have promised to be honest with you and with myself, so I repeat again that I embarked on this tragic venture merely through a rather overwrought desire to help, not through any other, any personal feeling, quite without any wishes or forebodings.

You must spare me the tale of what happened in that room that night; I myself have forgotten not a moment of it, and I never will. I spent it wrestling with another human being for his life, and I repeat, it was a battle of life and death. I felt only too clearly, with every fibre of my being, that this stranger, already half-lost, was clutching at his last chance with all the avid passion of a man threatened by death. He clung to me like one who already feels the abyss yawning beneath him. For my part, I summoned everything in me to save him by all the means at my command. A human being may know such an hour perhaps only once in his life, and out of millions, again, perhaps only one will know it—but for that terrible chance I myself would never have guessed how ardently, desperately, with what boundless greed a man given up for lost will still suck at every red drop of life. Kept safe for twenty years from all the demonic forces of existence, I would never have understood how magnificently, how fantastically Nature can merge hot and cold, life and death, delight and despair together in a few brief moments. And that night was so full of conflict and of talk, of passion and anger and hatred, with tears of entreaty and intoxication, that it seemed to me to last a thousand years, and we two human beings who fell entwined into its chasm, one of us in frenzy, the other unsuspecting, emerged from that mortal tumult changed, completely transformed, senses and emotions transmuted.

But I don't want to talk about that. I cannot and will not describe it. However, I must just tell you of the extraordinary moment when I woke in the morning from a leaden sleep, from nocturnal depths such as I had never known before. It took me a long time to open my eyes, and the first thing I saw was a strange ceiling over me, and then, looking further an entirely strange, unknown, ugly room. I had no idea how I came to be there. At first I told myself I must still be dreaming, an unusually lucid, transparent dream into which I had passed from my dull, confused slumber—but the sparkling bright sunshine outside the windows was unmistakably genuine, the light of morning, and the sounds of the street echoed from below, the rattle of carriages, the ringing of tram bells, the noise of people—so now I knew that I was awake and not dreaming. I instinctively sat up to get my bearings, and then—as my glance moved sideways—then I saw, and I can never describe my alarm to you, I saw a stranger sleeping in the broad bed beside me… a strange, perfectly strange, half-naked, unknown man… oh, I know there's no real way to describe the awful realisation; it struck me with such terrible force that I sank back powerless. But not in a kindly faint, not falling unconscious, far from it: with lightning speed, everything became as clear to me as it was inexplicable, and all I wanted was to die of revulsion and shame at suddenly finding myself in an unfamiliar bed in a decidedly shady hotel, with a complete stranger beside me. I still remember how my heart missed a beat, how I held my breath as if that would extinguish my life and above all my consciousness, which grasped everything yet understood none of it.

I shall never know how long I lay like that, all my limbs icy cold: the dead must lie rigid in their coffins in much the same way. All I know is that I had closed my eyes and was praying to God, to some heavenly power, that this might not be true, might not be real. But my sharpened senses would not let me deceive myself, I could hear people talking in the next room, water running, footsteps shuffling along the corridor outside, and each of these signs mercilessly proved that my senses were terribly alert.

How long this dreadful condition lasted I cannot say: such moments are outside the measured time of ordinary life. But suddenly another fear came over me, swift and terrible: the stranger whose name I did not know might wake up and speak to me. And I knew at once there was only one thing to do: I must get dressed and make my escape before he woke. I must not let him set eyes on me again, I must not speak to him again. I must save myself before it was too late, go away, away, away, back to some kind of life of my own, to my hotel, I must leave this pernicious place, leave this country, never meet him again, never look him in the eye, have no witnesses, no accusers, no one who knew. The idea dispelled my faintness: very cautiously, with the furtive movements of a thief, I inched out of bed (for I was desperate to make no noise) and groped my way over to my clothes. I dressed very carefully, trembling all the time lest he might wake up, and then I had finished, I had done it. Only my hat lay at the foot of the bed on the far side of the room, and then, as I tiptoed over to pick it up—I couldn't help it, at that moment I had to cast another glance at the face of the stranger who had fallen into my life like a stone dropping off a window sill. I meant it to be just one glance, but it was curious—the strange young man who lay sleeping there really was a stranger to me. At first I did not recognise his face from yesterday. The impassioned, tense, desperately distressed features of the mortally agitated man might have been entirely extinguished—this man's face was not the same, but was an utterly childlike, utterly boyish face that positively radiated purity and cheerfulness. The lips, so grim yesterday as he clenched his teeth on them, were dreaming, had fallen softly apart, half-curving in a smile; the fair hair curled gently over the smooth forehead, the breath passed from his chest over his body at repose like the mild rippling of waves.

Perhaps you may remember that I told you earlier I had never before seen greed and passion expressed with such outrageous extravagance by any human being as by that stranger at the gaming table. And I tell you now that I had never, even in children whose baby slumbers sometimes cast an angelic aura of cheerfulness around them, seen such an expression of brightness, of truly blissful sleep. The uniquely graphic nature of that face showed all its feelings, at present the paradisaical easing of all internal heaviness, a sense of freedom and salvation. At this surprising sight all my own fear and horror fell from me like a heavy black cloak—I was no longer ashamed, no, I was almost glad. The terrible and incomprehensible thing that had happened suddenly made sense to me; I was happy, I was proud to think that but for my dedicated efforts the beautiful, delicate young man lying here carefree and quiet as a flower would have been found somewhere on a rocky slope, his body shattered and bloody, his face ruined, lifeless, with staring eyes. I had saved him; he was safe. And now I looked—I cannot put it any other way—I looked with maternal feeling at the man I had reborn into life more painfully than I bore my own children. In the middle of that shabby, threadbare room in a distasteful, grubby house of assignation, I was overcome by the kind of emotion—ridiculous as you may find it put into words—the kind of emotion one might have in church, a rapturous sense of wonder and sanctification. From the most dreadful moment of a whole life there now grew a second life, amazing and overwhelming, coming in sisterly fashion to meet me.

Had I made too much noise moving about? Had I involuntarily exclaimed out loud? I don't know, but suddenly the sleeping man opened his eyes. I flinched back in alarm. He looked round in surprise—just as I had done before earlier, and now he in his own turn seemed to be emerging with difficulty from great depths of confusion. His gaze wandered intently round the strange, unfamiliar room and then fell on me in amazement. But before he spoke, or could quite pull himself together, I had control of myself. I did not let him say a word, I allowed no questions, no confidences; nothing of yesterday or of last night was to be explained, discussed or mulled over again.

'I have to go now,' I told him quickly. 'You stay here and get dressed. I'll meet you at twelve at the entrance to the casino, and I'll take care of everything else.'

And before he could say a word in reply I fled, to be rid of the sight of the room, and without turning back left the hotel whose name I did not know, any more than I knew the name of the stranger with whom I had just spent the night."

*

Mrs C interrupted her narrative for a moment again, but all the strain and distress had gone from her voice: like a carriage that toils uphill with difficulty but then, having reached the top, rolls swiftly and smoothly down the other side, her account now proceeded more easily:

"Well—so I made haste to my hotel through the morning light of the streets. The drop in the temperature had driven all the hazy mists from the sky above, just as my own distress had been dispelled. For remember what I told you earlier: I had given up my own life entirely after my husband's death. My children did not need me, I didn't care for my own company, and there's no point in a life lived aimlessly. Now, for the first time, a task had suddenly come my way: I had saved a human being, I had exerted all my powers to snatch him back from destruction. There was only a little left to do—for my task must be completed to the end. So I entered my hotel, ignoring the porter's surprise when he saw me returning at nine in the morning—no shame and chagrin over last night's events oppressed me now, I felt my will to live suddenly revive, and an unexpectedly new sense of the point of my existence flowed warmly through my veins. Once in my room I quickly changed my clothes, putting my mourning aside without thinking (as I noticed only later) and choosing a lighter colour instead, went to the bank to withdraw money, and made haste to the station to find out train times. With a determination that surprised me I also made a few other arrangements. Now there was nothing left to do but ensure the departure from Monte Carlo and ultimate salvation of the man whom fate had cast in my way.

It is true that I needed strength to face him personally. Everything yesterday had taken place in the dark, in a vortex; we had been like two stones thrown out of a torrential stream suddenly striking together; we scarcely knew each other face to face, and I wasn't even sure whether the stranger would recognise me again. Yesterday had been chance, frenzy, a case of two confused people possessed; today I must be more open with him, since I must now confront him in the pitiless light of day with myself, my own face, as a living human being.

But it all turned out much easier than I expected. No sooner had I approached the casino at the appointed hour than a young man jumped up from a bench and made haste towards me. There was something so spontaneous, so child-like, unplanned and happy in his surprise and in each of his eloquent movements; he almost flew to me, the radiance of a joy that was both grateful and deferential in his eyes, which were lowered humbly as soon as they felt my confusion in his presence. Gratitude is so seldom found, and those who are most grateful cannot express it, are silent in their confusion, or ashamed, or sometimes seem ungracious just to conceal their feelings. But in this man, the expression of whose every feeling God, like a mysterious sculptor, had made sensual, beautiful, graphic, his gratitude glowed with radiant passion right through his body. He bent over my hand and remained like that for a moment, the narrow line of his boyish head reverently bowed, respectfully brushing kisses on my fingers; only then did he step back, ask how I was, and look at me most movingly. There was such courtesy in everything he said that within a few minutes the last of my anxiety had gone. As if reflecting the lightening of my own feelings, the landscape around was shining, the spell on it broken: the sea that had been disturbed and angry yesterday lay so calm and bright that every pebble beneath the gently breaking surf gleamed white, and the casino, that den of iniquity, looked up with Moorish brightness to the damask sky that was now swept clean. The kiosk with the projecting roof beneath which the pouring rain had forced us to shelter yesterday proved to be a flower stall; great bunches of flowers and foliage lay there in motley confusion, in white, red, other bright colours and green, and a young girl in a colourful blouse was offering them for sale.

I invited him to lunch with me in a small restaurant, and there the young stranger told me the story of his tragic venture. It confirmed my first presentiment when I had seen his trembling, nervously shaking hands on the green table. He came from an old aristocratic family in the Austrian part of Poland, was destined for a diplomatic career, had studied in Vienna and passed his first examination with great success a month ago. As a reward, and to celebrate the occasion, his uncle, a high-ranking general-staff officer, had taken him to the Prater in a cab, and they went to the races. His uncle was lucky with his bets and won three times running; then they ate supper in an elegant restaurant on the strength of the fat wad of banknotes that were the uncle's gains. Next day, again to mark his success in the examinations, the budding diplomat received a sum of money from his father which was as much as his usual monthly allowance. Two days earlier this would have seemed to him a large sum, but now, seeing how easily his uncle had won money, it struck him as trifling and left him indifferent. Directly after dinner, therefore, he went to the races again, laid wild, frenzied bets, and fortune—or rather misfortune—would have it that he left the Prater after the last race with three times the sum he had brought there. Now a mania for gambling infected him; sometimes he went to the races, sometimes to play in coffee houses and clubs, exhausting his time, his studies, his nerves, and above all his money. He was no longer able to think or to sleep peacefully, and he was quite unable to control himself; one night, coming home from a club where he had lost everything, he found a crumpled banknote forgotten in his waistcoat pocket as he was undressing. There was no holding him; he got dressed again and walked the streets until he found a few people playing dominoes in a coffee house, and sat with them until dawn. On one occasion his married sister came to his aid, paying his debts to moneylenders who were very ready to give credit to the heir of a great and noble name. For a while he was lucky at play again—but then matters went inexorably downhill, and the more he lost, the more urgently did unsecured obligations and fixed-term IOUs require him to find relief by winning. He had long ago pawned his watch and his clothes, and at last a terrible thing happened: he stole two large pearl earrings that she seldom wore from his old aunt's dressing table. He pawned one of the pearls for a large sum, which his gambling quadrupled that evening. But instead of redeeming the pearl he staked all his winnings and lost. At the time when he left Vienna the theft had not yet been discovered, so he pawned the second pearl and on a sudden impulse travelled by train to Monte Carlo to win the fortune he dreamt of at roulette.

On arrival he had sold his suitcase, his clothes, his umbrella; he had nothing left but a revolver with four cartridges, and a small cross set with jewels given him by his godmother, Princess X. He did not want to part with the cross, but it too had been sold for fifty francs that afternoon, just to let him try to satisfy his urge by playing for life or death one last time that evening.

He told me all this with the captivating charm of his original and lively nature. And I listened shaken, gripped and much moved, but not for a moment did it occur to me to feel horror that the man at my table was in sober fact a thief. Yesterday, if someone had so much as suggested to me that I, a woman with a blameless past who expected the company she kept to be strictly and conventionally virtuous, would be sitting here on familiar terms with a perfectly strange young man, not much older than my son, who had stolen a pair of pearl earrings, I would have thought he had taken leave of his senses and such a thing was impossible. But I felt no horror at all as he told his tale, for he spoke so naturally and passionately that it seemed more like the account of a fever or illness than a crime. Moreover, the word 'impossible' had suddenly lost its meaning for a woman who had known such an unexpected, torrential experience as I had the night before. In those ten hours, I had come to know immeasurably more about reality than in my preceding forty respectable years of life.

Yet something else about his confession did alarm me, and that was the feverish glint in his eyes, which made all the nerves of his face twitch galvanically as he talked about his passion for gambling. Even speaking of it aroused him, and his face graphically and with terrible clarity illustrated that tension between pleasure and torment. His hands, those beautiful, nervous, slender-jointed hands, instinctively began to turn into preying, hunting, fleeing animal creatures again, just as they did at the gaming table. As he spoke I saw them suddenly trembling, beginning at the wrists, arching and clenching into fists, then opening up to intertwine their fingers once more. And when he confessed to the theft of the pearl earrings they suddenly performed a swift, leaping, quick, thieving movement—I involuntarily jumped. I could see his fingers pouncing on the jewels and swiftly stowing them away in the hollow of his clenched hand. And with nameless horror, I recognised that the very last drop of this man's blood was poisoned by his addiction.

That was the one thing that so shattered and horrified me about his tale, the pitiful enslavement of a young, light-hearted, naturally carefree man to a mad passion. I considered it my prime duty to persuade my unexpected protégé, in friendly fashion, that he must leave Monte Carlo, where the temptation was most dangerous, without delay, he must return to his family this very day, before anyone noticed that the pearl earrings were gone and his future was ruined for ever. I promised him money for his journey and to redeem the jewellery, though only on condition that he left today and swore to me, on his honour, never to touch a card or play any other game of chance again.

I shall never forget the passion of gratitude, humble at first, then gradually more ardent, with which that lost stranger listened to me, how he positively drank in my words as I promised him help, and then he suddenly reached both hands over the table to take mine in a gesture I can never forget, a gesture of what one might call adoration and sacred promise. There were tears in his bright but slightly confused eyes; his whole body was trembling nervously with happy excitement. I have tried to describe the uniquely expressive quality of his gestures to you several times already, but I cannot depict this one, for it conveyed ecstatic, supernal delight such as a human countenance seldom turns on us, comparable only to that white shade in which, waking from a dream, we think we see the countenance of an angel vanishing.

Why conceal it? I could not withstand that glance. Gratitude is delightful because it is so seldom found, tender feeling does one good, and such exuberance was delightfully new and heart-warming to me, sober, cool woman that I was. And with that crushed, distressed young man, the landscape itself had revived as if by magic after last night's rain. The sea, calm as a millpond, lay shining blue beneath the sky as we came out of the restaurant, and the only white to be seen was the white of seagulls swooping in that other, celestial blue. You know the Riviera landscape. It is always beautiful, but offers its rich colours to the eye in leisurely fashion, flat as a picture postcard, a lethargic sleeping beauty who admits all glances, imperturbable and almost oriental in her ever-opulent willingness. But sometimes, very occasionally, there are days when this beauty rises up, breaks out, cries out loud, you might say, with gaudy, fanatically sparkling colours, triumphantly flinging her flower-like brightness in your face, glowing, burning with sensuality. And the stormy chaos of the night before had turned to such a lively day, the road was washed white, the sky was turquoise, and everywhere bushes ignited like colourful torches among the lush, drenched green foliage. The mountains seemed suddenly lighter and closer in the cooler, sunny air, as if they were crowding towards the gleaming, polished little town out of curiosity. Stepping outside, you sensed at every glance the challenging, cheering aspect of Nature spontaneously drawing your heart to her. 'Let's hire a carriage and drive along the Corniche,' I said.

The young man nodded enthusiastically: he seemed to be really seeing and noticing the landscape for the first time since his arrival. All he had seen so far was the dank casino hall with its sultry, sweaty smell, its crowds of ugly visitors with their twisted features, and a rough, grey, clamorous sea outside. But now the sunny beach lay spread out before us like a huge fan, and the eye leapt with pleasure from one distant point to another. We drove along the beautiful road in a slow carriage (this was before the days of the motor car), past many villas and many fine views; a hundred times, seeing every house, every villa in the green shade of the pine trees, one felt a secret wish to live there, quiet and content, away from the world!

Was I ever happier in my life than in that hour? I don't know. Beside me in the carriage sat the young man who had been a prey to death and disaster yesterday and now, in amazement, stood in the spray of the sparkling white dome of the sun above; years seemed to have dropped away from him. He had become all boy, a handsome, sportive child with a playful yet respectful look in his eyes, and nothing about him delighted me more than his considerate attentiveness. If the carriage was going up a steep climb which the horses found arduous, he jumped nimbly down to push from behind. If I named a flower or pointed to one by the roadside, he hurried to pluck it. He picked up a little toad that was hopping with difficulty along the road, lured out by last night's rain, and carried it carefully over to the green grass, where it would not be crushed as the carriage went by; and from time to time, in great high spirits, he would say the most delightful and amusing things; I believe he found laughter of that kind a safety valve, and without it he would have had to sing or dance or fool around in some way, so happily inebriated was the expression of his sudden exuberance.

As we were driving slowly through a tiny village high up on the road, he suddenly raised his hat politely. I was surprised and asked who he was greeting, since he was a stranger among strangers here. He flushed slightly at my question and explained, almost apologetically, that we had just passed a church, and at home in Poland, as in all strict Catholic countries, it was usual from childhood on to raise your hat outside any church or other place of worship. I was deeply moved by this exquisite respect for religion, and remembering the cross he had mentioned, I asked if he was a devout believer. When he modestly confessed, with a touch of embarrassment, that he hoped to be granted God's grace, an idea suddenly came to me. 'Stop!' I told the driver, and quickly climbed out of the carriage. He followed me in surprise, asking, 'Where are we going?' I said only, 'Come with me.'

In his company I went back to the church, a small country church built of brick. The interior looked chalky, grey and empty; the door stood open, so that a yellow beam of light cut sharply through the dark, where blue shadows surrounded a small altar. Two candles, like veiled eyes, looked out of the warm, incense-scented twilight. We entered, he took off his hat, dipped his hand in the basin of holy water, crossed himself and genuflected. When he was standing again I took his arm. 'Go and find an altar or some image here that is holy to you,' I urged him, 'and swear the oath I will recite to you.' He looked at me in surprise, almost in alarm. But quickly understanding, he went over to a niche, made the sign of the cross and obediently knelt down. 'Say after me,' I said, trembling with excitement myself, 'say after me: I swear…'—'I swear,' he repeated, and I continued, 'that I will never play for money again, whatever the game may be, I swear that I will never again expose my life and my honour to the dangers of that passion.'

He repeated the words, trembling: they lingered loud and clear in the empty interior. Then it was quiet for a moment, so quiet that you could hear the faint rustling of the trees outside as the wind blew through their leaves. Suddenly he threw himself down like a penitent and, in tones of ecstasy such as I had never heard before, poured out a flood of rapid, confused words in Polish. I did not understand what he was saying, but it was obviously an ecstatic prayer, a prayer of gratitude and remorse, for in his stormy confession he kept bowing his head humbly down on the prayer desk, repeating the strange sounds ever more passionately, and uttering the same word more and more violently and with extraordinary ardour. I have never heard prayer like that before or since, in any church in the world. As he prayed his hands clung convulsively to the wooden prayer desk, his whole body shaken by an internal storm that sometimes caught him up and sometimes cast him down again. He saw and felt nothing else: his whole being seemed to exist in another world, in a purgatorial fire of transmutation, or rising to a holier sphere. At last he slowly stood up, made the sign of the cross, and turned with an effort. His knees were trembling, his countenance was pale as the face of a man exhausted. But when he saw me his eyes beamed, a pure, a truly devout smile lit up his ecstatic face; he came closer, bowed low in the Russian manner, took both my hands and touched them reverently with his lips. 'God has sent you to me. I was thanking him.' I did not know what to say, but I could have wished the organ to crash out suddenly above the low pews, for I felt that I had succeeded: I had saved this man for ever.

We emerged from the church into the radiant, flooding light of that May-like day; the world had never before seemed to me more beautiful. Then we drove slowly on in the carriage for another two hours, taking the panoramic road over the hills which offers a new view at every turn. But we spoke no more. After so much emotion, any other words would have seemed an anti-climax. And when by chance my eyes met his, I had to turn them away as if ashamed, so shaken was I by the sight of my own miracle.

We returned to Monte Carlo at about five in the afternoon. I had an appointment with relatives which I could not cancel at this late date. And in fact I secretly wished for a pause in which to recover from feelings that had been too violently aroused. For this was too much happiness. I felt that I must rest from my overheated, ecstatic condition. I had never known anything like it in my life before. So I asked my protégé to come into my hotel with me for a moment, and there in my room I gave him the money for his journey and to redeem the jewellery. We agreed that while I kept my appointment he would go and buy his ticket, and then we would meet at seven in the entrance hall of the station, half-an-hour before the departure of the train taking him home by way of Genoa. When I was about to give him the five banknotes his lips turned curiously pale. 'No… no money… I beg you, not money!' he uttered through his teeth, while his agitated fingers quivered nervously. 'No money… not money… I can't stand the sight of it!' he repeated, as if physically overcome by nausea or fear. But I soothed him, saying it was only a loan, and if he felt troubled by it then he could give me a receipt. 'Yes, yes… a receipt,' he murmured, looking away, cramming the crumpled notes into his pocket without looking at them, like something sticky that soiled his fingers, and he scribbled a couple of words on a piece of paper in swift, flying characters. When he looked up damp sweat was standing out on his brow; something within seemed to be choking him, and no sooner had he given me the note than an impulse seemed to pass through him and suddenly—I was so startled that I instinctively flinched back—suddenly he fell on his knees and kissed the hem of my dress. It was an indescribable gesture; its overwhelming violence made me tremble all over. A strange shuddering came over me; I was confused, and could only stammer, 'Thank you for showing your gratitude—but do please go now! We'll say goodbye at seven in the station hall.'

He looked at me with a gleam of emotion moistening his eye; for a moment I thought he was going to say something, for a moment it seemed as if he were coming towards me. But then he suddenly bowed deeply again, very deeply, and left the room."

Once again Mrs C interrupted her story. She had risen and gone to the window to look out, and she stood there motionless for a long time. Watching the silhouette of her back, I saw it shiver slightly, and she swayed. All at once she turned back to me with determination, and her hands, until now calm and at rest, suddenly made a violent, tearing movement as if to rip something apart. Then she looked at me with a hard, almost defiant glance, and abruptly began again.

"I promised to be completely honest with you, and now I see how necessary that promise was. For only now that, for the first time, I make myself describe the whole course of those hours exactly as they happened, seeking words for what was a very complicated, confused feeling, only now do I clearly understand much that I did not know at the time, or perhaps would not acknowledge. So I will be firm and will not spare myself, and I will tell you the truth too: then, at the moment when the young man left the room and I remained there alone, I felt—it was a dazed sensation, like swooning—I felt a hard blow strike my heart. Something had hurt me mortally, but I did not know, or refused to know, what, after all, it was in my protégé's touchingly respectful conduct that wounded me so painfully.

But now that I force myself to bring up all the past unsparingly, in proper order, as if it were strange to me, and your presence as a witness allows no pretence, no craven concealment of a feeling which shames me, I clearly see that what hurt so much at the time was disappointment... my disappointment that... that the young man had gone away so obediently... that he did not try to detain me, to stay with me. It was because he humbly and respectfully fell in with my first attempt to persuade him to leave, instead... instead of trying to take me in his arms. It was because he merely revered me as a saint who had appeared to him along his way and did not... did not feel for me as a woman.

That was the disappointment I felt, a disappointment I did not admit to myself either then or later, but a woman's feelings know everything without words, without conscious awareness. For—and now I will deceive myself no longer—for if he had embraced me then, if he had asked me then, I would have gone to the ends of the earth with him, I would have dishonoured my name and the name of my children—I would have eloped with him, caring nothing for what people would say or the dictates of my own reason, just as Madame Henriette ran off with the young Frenchman whom she hadn't even met the day before. I wouldn't have asked where we were going, or how long it would last, I wouldn't have turned to look back at my previous life—I would have sacrificed my money, my name, my fortune and my honour to him, I would have begged in the street for him, there is probably no base conduct in the world to which he could not have brought me. I would have thrown away all that we call modesty and reason if he had only spoken one word, taken one step towards me, if he had tried to touch me—so lost in him was I at that moment. But... as I told you... the young man, in his strangely dazed condition, did not spare another glance for me and the woman in me... and I knew how much, how fervently I longed for him only when I was alone again, when the passion that had just been lighting up his radiant, his positively seraphic face was cast darkly back on me and now lingered in the void of an abandoned breast. With difficulty, I pulled myself together. My appointment was a doubly unwelcome burden. I felt as if a heavy iron helmet were weighing down on my brow and I was swaying under its weight; my thoughts were as disjointed as my footsteps as I at last went over to the other hotel to see my relatives. I sat there in a daze, amidst lively chatter, and was startled whenever I happened to look up and see their unmoved faces, which seemed to me frozen like masks by comparison with that face of his, enlivened as if by the play of light and shade as clouds cross the sky. I found the cheerful company as dreadfully inert as if I were among the dead, and while I put sugar in my cup and joined absently in the conversation, that one face kept coming before my mind's eye, as if summoned up by the surging of the blood. It had become a fervent joy to me to watch that face, and—terrible thought!—in an hour or so I would have seen it for the last time. I must involuntarily have sighed or groaned gently, for my husband's cousin leant over to me: what was the matter, she asked, didn't I feel well? I looked so pale and sad. This unexpected question gave me a quick, easy excuse; I said I did indeed have a migraine, and perhaps she would allow me to slip away.

Thus restored to my own company, I hurried straight to my hotel. No sooner was I alone there than the sense of emptiness and abandonment came over me again, feverishly combined with a longing for the young man I was to leave today for ever. I paced up and down the room, opened shutters for no good reason, changed my dress and my ribbon, suddenly found myself in front of the looking glass again, wondering whether, thus adorned, I might not be able to attract him after all. And I abruptly understood myself: I would do anything not to lose him! Within the space of a violent moment, my wish turned to determination. I ran down to the porter and told him I was leaving today by the night train. Now I had to hurry: I rang for the maid to help me pack—time was pressing—and as we stowed dresses and small items into my suitcases I dreamt of the coming surprise: I would accompany him to the train, and then, at the very last moment, when he was giving me his hand in farewell, I would suddenly get into the carriage with my astonished companion, I would spend that night with him, and the next night—as long as he wanted me. A kind of enchanted, wild frenzy whirled through my blood, sometimes, to the maid's surprise, I unexpectedly laughed aloud as I flung clothes into the suitcases. My senses, I felt from time to time, were all in disorder. And when the man came to take the cases down I stared at him strangely at first: it was too difficult to think of ordinary matters while I was in the grip of such inner excitement.

Time was short; it must be nearly seven, leaving me at most twenty minutes before the train left—but of course, I consoled myself, my arrival would not be a farewell now, since I had decided to accompany him on his journey as long and as far as he would have me. The hotel manservant carried the cases on ahead while I made haste to the reception desk to settle my bill. The manager was already giving me change, I was about to go on my way, when a hand gently touched my shoulder. I gave a start. It was my cousin; concerned by my apparent illness, she had come to see how I was. Everything went dark before my eyes. I did not want her here; every second I was detained meant disastrous delay, yet courtesy obliged me at least to fall into conversation with her briefly. 'You must go to bed,' she was urging me. 'I'm sure you have a temperature.' And she could well have been right, for the blood was pounding at my temples, and sometimes I felt the blue haze of approaching faintness come over my eyes. But I fended off her suggestions and took pains to seem grateful, while every word burned me, and I would have liked to thrust her ill-timed concern roughly away. However, she stayed and stayed and stayed with her unwanted solicitude, offered me eau de Cologne, would not be dissuaded from dabbing the cool perfume on my temples herself. Meanwhile I was counting the minutes, thinking both of him and of how to find an excuse to escape the torment of her sympathy. And the more restless I became, the more alarming did my condition seem to her; finally she was trying, almost by force, to make me go to my room and lie down. Then—in the middle of her urging—I suddenly saw the clock in the hotel lobby: it was two minutes before seven-thirty, and the train left at seven thirty-five. Brusquely, abruptly, with the brutal indifference of a desperate woman I simply stuck my hand out to my cousin—'Goodbye, I must go!'—and without a moment's thought for her frozen glance, without looking round, I rushed past the surprised hotel staff and out of the door, into the street and down it to the station. From the agitated gesticulating of the hotel manservant standing waiting there with my luggage I saw, well before I got there, that time must be very short. Frantically I ran to the barrier, but there the conductor turned me back—I had forgotten to buy a ticket. And as I almost forcibly tried to persuade him to let me on the platform all the same, the train began to move. I stared at it, trembling all over, hoping at least to catch a glimpse of him at the window of one of the carriages, a wave, a greeting. But in the middle of the hurrying throng I could not see his face. The carriages rolled past faster and faster, and after a minute nothing was left before my darkened eyes but black clouds of steam.

I must have stood there as if turned to stone, for God knows how long; the hotel servant had probably spoken to me in vain several times before he ventured to touch my arm. Only then did I start and come to myself. Should he take my luggage back to the hotel, he asked. It took me a few minutes to think; no, that was impossible, after this ridiculous, frantic departure I couldn't go back there, and I never wanted to again; so I told him, impatient to be alone, to take my cases to the left luggage office. Only then, in the middle of the constantly renewed crush of people flowing clamorously into the hall and then ebbing away again, did I try to think, to think clearly, to save myself from my desperate, painful, choking sense of fury, remorse and despair, for—why not admit it?—the idea that I had missed our last meeting through my own fault was like a knife turning pitilessly within me, burning and sharp. I could have screamed aloud: that red-hot blade, penetrating ever more mercilessly, hurt so much. Perhaps only those who are strangers to passion know such sudden outbursts of emotion in their few passionate moments, moments of emotion like an avalanche or a hurricane; whole years fall from one's own breast with the fury of powers left unused. Never before or after have I felt anything like the astonishment and raging impotence of that moment when, prepared to take the boldest of steps—prepared to throw away my whole carefully conserved, collected, controlled life all at once—I suddenly found myself facing a wall of senselessness against which my passion could only beat its head helplessly.

As for what I did then, how could it be anything but equally senseless? It was foolish, even stupid, and I am almost ashamed to tell you—but I have promised myself and you to keep nothing back. I… well, I went in search of him again. That is to say, I went in search of every moment I had spent with him. I felt irresistibly drawn to everywhere we had been together the day before, the bench in the casino grounds from which I had made him rise, the gaming hall where I had first seen him—yes, even that den of vice, just to relive the past once more, only once more. And tomorrow I would go along the Corniche in a carriage, retracing our path, so that every word and gesture would revive in my mind again—so senseless and childish was my state of confusion. But you must take into account the lightning speed with which these events overwhelmed me—I had felt little more than a single numbing blow, but now, woken too abruptly from that tumult of feeling,

I wanted to go back over what I had so fleetingly experienced step by step, relishing it in retrospect by virtue of that magical self-deception we call memory. Well, some things we either do or do not understand. Perhaps you need a burning heart to comprehend them fully.

So I went first to the gaming hall to seek out the table where he had been sitting, and think of his hands among all the others there. I went in: I remembered that I had first seen him at the left-hand table in the second room. Every one of his movements was still clear before my mind's eye: I could have found his place sleepwalking, with my eyes closed and my hands outstretched. So I went in and crossed the hall. And then... as I looked at the crowd from the doorway... then something strange happened. There, in the very place where I dreamt of him, there sat—ah, the hallucinations of fever!—there sat the man himself. He looked exactly as I had seen him in my daydream just now—exactly as he had been yesterday, his eyes fixed on the ball, pale as a ghost—but he it unmistakably was.

I was so shocked that I felt as if I must cry out. But I controlled my alarm at this ridiculous vision and closed my eyes. 'You're mad—dreaming—feverish,' I told myself. 'It's impossible. You're hallucinating. He left half-an-hour ago.' Only then did I open my eyes again. But terrible to relate, he was still sitting there exactly as he had been sitting just now, in the flesh and unmistakable. I would have known those hands among millions... no, I wasn't dreaming, he was real. He had not left as he had promised he would, the madman was sitting there, he had taken the money I gave him for his journey and brought it here, to the green table, gambling it on his passion, oblivious of all else, while I was desperately eating my heart out for him.

I abruptly moved forwards: fury blurred my vision, a frenzied, red-eyed, raging desire to take the perjurer who had so shamefully abused my confidence, my feelings, my devotion by the throat. But I controlled myself. With a deliberately slow step (and how much strength that cost me!) I went up to the table to sit directly opposite him. A gentleman courteously made way for me. Two metres of green cloth stood between us, and as if looking down from a balcony at a play on stage I could watch his face, the same face that I had seen two hours ago radiant with gratitude, illuminated by the aura of divine grace, and now entirely absorbed in the infernal fires of his passion again. The hands, those same hands that I had seen clinging to the wood of the prayer desk as he swore a most sacred oath, were now clutching at the money again like the claws of lustful vampires. For he had been winning, he must have won a very great deal: in front of him shone a jumbled pile of jettons and louis d'ors and banknotes, a disordered medley in which his quivering, nervous fingers were stretching and bathing with delight. I saw them pick up separate notes, stroke and fold them, I saw them turn and caress coins, then suddenly and abruptly catch up a fistful and put them down on one of the spaces. And immediately that spasmodic tic around his nostrils began again, the call of the croupier tore his greedily blazing eyes away from the money to the spinning ball, he seemed to be flowing out of himself, as it were, while his elbows might have been nailed to the green table. His total addiction was revealed as even more dreadful, more terrible than the evening before, for every move he made murdered that other image within me, the image shining as if on a golden ground that I had credulously swallowed.

So we sat there two metres away from each other; I was staring at him, but he was unaware of me. He was not looking at me or anyone else, his glance merely moved to the money, flickering unsteadily with the ball as it rolled back to rest: all his senses were contained, chasing back and forth, in that one racing green circle. To this obsessive gambler the whole world, the whole human race had shrunk to a rectangular patch of cloth. And I knew that I could stand here for hours and hours, and he would not have the faintest idea of my presence.

But I could stand it no longer. Coming to a sudden decision, I walked round the table, stepped behind him and firmly grasped his shoulder with my hand. His gaze swung upwards, for a second he stared strangely at me, glassy-eyed, like a drunk being laboriously shaken awake, eyes still vague and drowsy, clouded by inner fumes. Then he seemed to recognise me, his mouth opened, quivering, he looked happily up at me and stammered quietly, in a confused tone of mysterious confidentiality, 'It's going well… I knew it would as soon as I came in and saw that he was here…' I did not understand what he meant. All I saw was that this madman was intoxicated by the game and had forgotten everything else, his promise, his appointment at the station, me and the whole world besides. But even when he was in this obsessive mood I found his ecstasy so captivating that instinctively I went along with him and asked, taken aback, who was here?

'Over there, the one-armed old Russian general,' he whispered, pressing close to me so that no one else would overhear the magic secret. 'Over there, with the white sideboards and the servant behind him. He always wins, I was watching him yesterday, he must have a system, and I always pick the same number... He was winning yesterday too, but I made the mistake of playing on when he had left... that was my error... he must have won twenty thousand francs yesterday, he's winning every time now too, and I just keep following his lead. Now—'

He broke off in mid-sentence, for the hoarse-voiced croupier was calling his '*Faites votre jeu!*' and his glance was already moving away, looking greedily at the place where the white-whiskered Russian sat, nonchalant and grave, thoughtfully putting first one gold coin and then, hesitantly, another on the fourth space. Immediately the fevered hands before me dug into the pile of money and put down a handful of coins on the same place. And when, after a minute, the croupier cried '*Zéro!*' and his rake swept the whole table bare with a single movement, he stared at the money streaming away as if at some marvel. But do you think he turned to me? No he had forgotten all about me; I had dropped out of his life, I was lost and gone from it, his whole being was intent only on the Russian general who, with complete indifference, was hefting two more gold coins in his hand, not yet sure what number to put them on.

I cannot describe my bitterness and despair. But think of my feelings: to be no more than a fly brushed carelessly aside by a man to whom one has offered one's whole life. Once again that surge of fury came over me. I seized his arm with all my strength. He started.

'You will get up at once!' I whispered to him in a soft but commanding tone. 'Remember what you swore in church today, you miserable perjurer.'

He stared at me, perplexed and pale. His eyes suddenly took on the expression of a beaten dog, his lips quivered. All at once he seemed to be remembering the past, and a horror of himself appeared to come over him.

'Yes, yes…' he stammered. 'Oh, my God, my God… yes, I'm coming, oh, forgive me…'

And his hand was already sweeping the money together, fast at first, gathering it all up with a vehement gesture, but then gradually slowing down, as if coming up against some opposing force. His eyes had fallen once more on the Russian general, who had just made his bet.

'Just a moment,' he said, quickly throwing five gold coins on the same square. 'Just this one more time… I promise you I'll come then—just this one more game… just…'

And again his voice fell silent. The ball had begun to roll and was carrying him away with it. Once again the addict had slipped away from me, from himself, flung round with the tiny ball circling in the smooth hollow of the wheel where it leapt and sprang. Once again the croupier called out the number, once again the rake carried his five coins away from him; he had lost. But he did not turn round. He had forgotten me, just like his oath in the church and the promise he had given me a minute ago. His greedy hand was moving spasmodically towards the dwindling pile of money again, and his intoxicated gaze moved only to the magnet of his will, the man opposite who brought good luck.

My patience was at an end. I shook him again, hard this time. 'Get up at once! Immediately! You said one more game…'

But then something unexpected happened. He suddenly swung round, but the face looking at me was no longer that of a humbled and confused man, it was the face of a man in a frenzy, all anger, with burning eyes and furiously trembling lips. 'Leave me alone!' he spat. 'Go away! You bring me bad luck. Whenever you're here I lose. You brought bad luck yesterday and you're bringing bad luck now. Go away!'

I momentarily froze, but now my own anger was whipped up beyond restraint by his folly.

'I am bringing you bad luck?' I snapped at him. 'You liar, you thief—you promised me…' But I got no further, for the maniac leapt up from his seat and, indifferent to the turmoil around him, thrust me away. 'Leave me alone,' he cried, losing all control. 'I'm not under your control… here, take your money.' And he threw me a few hundred-franc notes. 'Now leave me alone!'

He had been shouting out loud like a madman, ignoring the hundred or so people around us. They were all staring, whispering, pointing, laughing—other curious onlookers even crowded in from the hall next door. I felt as if my clothes were being torn from my body, leaving me naked before all these prying eyes. '*Silence, madame, s'il vous plaît,*' said the croupier in commanding tones, tapping his rake on the table. He meant me, the wretched creature meant me. Humiliated, overcome by shame, I stood there before the hissing, whispering curious folk like a prostitute whose customer has just thrown money at her. Two hundred, three hundred shameless eyes were turned on my face, and then—then, as I turned my gaze evasively aside, overwhelmed by this filthy deluge of humiliation and shame, my own eyes met two others, piercing and astonished—it was my cousin looking at me appalled, her mouth open, one hand raised as if in horror.

That struck home; before she could stir or recover from her surprise I stormed out of the hall. I got as far as the bench outside, the same bench on which the gambling addict had collapsed yesterday. I dropped to the hard, pitiless wood, as powerless, exhausted and shattered as he had been.

All that is twenty-four years ago, yet when I remember the moment when I stood there before a thousand strangers, lashed by their scorn, the blood freezes in my veins. And once again I feel, in horror, how weak, poor and flabby a substance whatever we call by the names of soul, spirit or feeling must be after all, not to mention what we describe as pain, since all this, even to the utmost degree, is insufficient to destroy the suffering flesh of the tormented body entirely—for we do survive such hours and our blood continues to pulse, instead of dying and falling like a tree struck by lightning. Only for a sudden moment, for an instant, did this pain tear through my joints so hard that I dropped on the bench breathless and dazed, with a positively voluptuous premonition that I must die. But as I was saying, pain is cowardly, it gives way before the overpowering will to live which seems to cling more strongly to our flesh than all the mortal suffering of the spirit. Even to myself, I cannot explain my feelings after such a shattering blow, but I did rise to my feet, although I did not know what to do. Suddenly it occurred to me that my suitcases were already at the station, and I thought suddenly that I must get away, away from here, away from this accursed, this infernal building. Taking no notice of anyone, I made haste to the station and asked when the next train for Paris left. At ten o'clock, the porter told me, and I immediately retrieved my luggage. Ten o'clock—so exactly twenty-four hours had passed since that terrible meeting, twenty-four hours so full of changeable, contradictory feelings that my inner world was shattered for ever. At first, however, I felt nothing but that one word in the constantly hammering, pounding rhythm: away, away, away! The pulses behind my brow kept driving it into my temples like a wedge: away, away, away! Away from this town, away from myself, home to my own people, to my own old life! I travelled through the night to Paris, changed from one station to another and travelled direct to Boulogne, from Boulogne to Dover, from Dover to London, from London to my son's house—all in one headlong flight, without stopping to think or consider, forty-eight hours without sleep, without speaking to anyone, without eating, forty-eight hours during which the wheels of all the trains rattled out that one word: away, away, away! When at last I arrived unexpectedly at my son's country house, everyone was alarmed; there must have been something in my bearing and my eyes that gave me away. My son came to embrace and kiss me, but I shrank away: I could not bear the thought of his touching lips that I felt were disgraced. I avoided all questions, asked only for a bath, because I needed to wash not only the dirt of the journey from my body but all of the passion of that obsessed, unworthy man that seemed to cling to it. Then I dragged myself up to my room and slept a benumbed and stony sleep for twelve or fourteen hours, a sleep such as I have never slept before or since, and after it I know what it must be like to lie dead in a coffin. My family cared for me as for a sick woman, but their affection only hurt me, I was ashamed of their respect, and had to keep preventing myself from suddenly screaming out loud how I had betrayed, forgotten and abandoned them all for the sake of a foolish, crazy passion.

Then, aimless again, I went back to France and a little town where I knew no one, for I was pursued by the delusion that at the very first glance everyone could see my shame and my changed nature from the outside, I felt so betrayed, so soiled to the depths of my soul. Sometimes, when I woke in my bed in the morning, I felt a dreadful fear of opening my eyes. Once again I would be overcome by the memory of that night when I suddenly woke beside a half-naked stranger, and then, as I had before, all I wanted was to die immediately.

But after all, time is strong, and age has the curious power of devaluing all our feelings. You feel death coming closer, its shadow falls black across your path, and things seem less brightly coloured, they do not go to the heart so much, they lose much of their dangerous violence. Gradually I recovered from the shock, and when, many years later, I met a young Pole who was an attaché of the Austrian Embassy at a party, and in answer to my enquiry about that family he told me that one of his cousin's sons had shot himself ten years before in Monte Carlo, I did not even tremble. It hardly hurt any more;

perhaps—why deny one's egotism?—I was even glad of it, for now my last fear of ever meeting him again was gone. I had no witness against me left but my own memory. Since then I have become calmer. Growing old, after all, means that one no longer fears the past.

And now you will understand why I suddenly brought myself to tell you about my own experience. When you defended Madame Henriette and said, so passionately, that twenty-four hours could determine a woman's whole life, I felt that you meant me; I was grateful to you, since for the first time I felt myself, as it were, confirmed in my existence. And then I thought it would be good to unburden myself of it all for once, and perhaps then the spell on me would be broken, the eternal looking back; perhaps I can go to Monte Carlo tomorrow and enter the same hall where I met my fate without feeling hatred for him or myself. Then the stone will roll off my soul, laying its full weight over the past and preventing it from ever rising again. It has done me good to tell you all this. I feel easier in my mind now and almost light at heart... thank you for that."

With these words she had suddenly risen, and I felt that she had reached the end. Rather awkwardly, I sought for something to say. But she must have felt my emotion, and quickly waved it away.

"No, please, don't speak... I'd rather you didn't reply or say anything to me. Accept my thanks for listening, and I wish you a good journey."

She stood opposite me, holding out her hand in farewell. Instinctively I looked at her face, and the countenance of this old woman who stood before me with a kindly yet slightly ashamed expression seemed to me wonderfully touching. Whether it was the reflection of past passion or mere confusion that suddenly dyed her cheeks with red, the colour rising to her white hair, she stood there just like a girl, in a bridal confusion of memories and ashamed of her own confession. Involuntarily moved, I very much wanted to say something to express my respect for her, but my throat was too constricted. So I leant down and respectfully kissed the faded hand that trembled slightly like an autumn leaf.

STEFAN ZWEIG was born in 1881 in Vienna, into a wealthy Austrian-Jewish family. He studied in Berlin and Vienna and first became known as a poet and translator, then as a biographer. Zweig travelled widely, living in Salzburg between the wars, and was an international bestseller with a string of hugely popular novellas including *Twenty-four Hours in the Life of a Woman, Letter from an Unknown Woman, Amok* and *Fear*. In 1934, with the rise of Nazism, he moved to London, where he wrote his only finished novel, *Beware of Pity*, and later on to Bath, taking British citizenship after the outbreak of the Second World War. With the fall of France in 1940 Zweig left Britain for New York, before settling in Brazil, where in 1942 he and his wife were found dead in an apparent double suicide. He had posted the manuscript of *The World of Yesterday* to his publisher the previous day. Much of Stefan Zweig's work is available from Pushkin Press.

Pushkin Press

Pushkin Press was founded in 1997, and publishes novels, essays, memoirs, children's books—everything from timeless classics to the urgent and contemporary.

Our books represent exciting, high-quality writing from around the world: we publish some of the twentieth century's most widely acclaimed, brilliant authors such as Stefan Zweig, Marcel Aymé, Antal Szerb, Paul Morand and Yasushi Inoue, as well as compelling and award-winning contemporary writers, including Andrés Neuman, Edith Pearlman and Ryu Murakami.

Pushkin Press publishes the world's best stories, to be read and read again. Here are just some of the titles from our long and varied list:

THE SPECTRE OF ALEXANDER WOLF

GAITO GAZDANOV

'A mesmerising work of literature' Antony Beevor

BINOCULAR VISION

EDITH PEARLMAN

'A genius of the short story' Mark Lawson, *Guardian*

TRAVELLER OF THE CENTURY

ANDRÉS NEUMAN

'A beautiful, accomplished novel: as ambitious as it is generous, as moving as it is smart' Juan Gabriel Vásquez, *Guardian*

BEWARE OF PITY

STEFAN ZWEIG

'Zweig's fictional masterpiece' *Guardian*

THE BREAK

PIETRO GROSSI

'Small and perfectly formed… reaching its end leaves the reader desirous to start all over again' *Independent*

FROM THE FATHERLAND, WITH LOVE

RYU MURAKAMI

'If Haruki is *The Beatles* of Japanese literature, Ryu is its *Rolling Stones*' David Pilling

BUTTERFLIES IN NOVEMBER

AUÐUR AVA ÓLAFSDÓTTIR

'A funny, moving and occasionally bizarre exploration of life's upheavals and reversals' *Financial Times*

BARCELONA SHADOWS

MARC PASTOR

'As gruesome as it is gripping… the writing is extraordinarily vivid… Highly recommended' *Independent*

THE LAST DAYS

LAURENT SEKSIK

'Mesmerising… Seksik's portrait of Zweig's final months is dignified and tender' *Financial Times*

BY BLOOD

ELLEN ULLMAN

'Delicious and intriguing' *Daily Telegraph*

WHILE THE GODS WERE SLEEPING

ERWIN MORTIER

'A monumental, phenomenal book' *De Morgen*

THE BRETHREN

ROBERT MERLE

'A master of the historical novel' *Guardian*

THE
SOCIETY
of the
CROSSED
KEYS